A STUDY GUIDE TO GENESIS 1

Genesis 1

The Design and Plan for the Kingdom of Heaven

A

THE BEGINNING

DANA GEORGE COTTRELL

WestBow
PRESS

Scripture quotations are from the New King James Version. Copyright © 1979, 1980, 1982, Thomas Nelson Inc., Publishers

WestBow Press books may be ordered through booksellers or by contacting:

WestBow Press
A Division of Thomas Nelson
1663 Liberty Drive
Bloomington, IN 47403
www.westbowpress.com
1-(866) 928-1240

Because of the dynamic nature of the Internet, any Web addresses or links contained in this book may have changed since publication and may no longer be valid. The views expressed in this work are solely those of the author and do not necessarily reflect the views of the publisher, and the publisher hereby disclaims any responsibility for them.

ISBN: 978-1-4497-0196-3 (sc)
ISBN: 978-1-4497-0197-0 (hc)
ISBN: 978-1-4497-0195-6 (e)

Library of Congress Control Number: 2010926337

Pencil portrait of author by Albert Coria

Printed in the United States of America

WestBow Press rev. date: 5/11/2010

To my wife Penny
and
to those who hunger to know and understand the holy Scriptures

Contents

Foreword

Jesus and John the Baptist began their ministry preaching repentance and proclaiming that the kingdom of heaven was at hand:

> In those days John the Baptist came preaching in the wilderness of Judea, and saying, "Repent, for the kingdom of heaven is at hand!" (Matthew 3:1, 2)

> From that time Jesus began to preach and to say, "Repent, for the kingdom of heaven is at hand." (Matthew 4:17)

When Jesus later sent out the twelve apostles, He told them to proclaim that the kingdom of heaven was at hand:

> These twelve Jesus sent out and commanded them, saying "… And as you go, preach, saying, 'The kingdom of heaven is at hand.'" (Matthew 10:5–7)

The kingdom of heaven was so prominent in Christ's message that the term is mentioned more than thirty times in Matthew's gospel. Jesus, either directly or indirectly through others, was introducing the kingdom of heaven. He, along with His followers, were preaching the gospel—glad tidings of the kingdom.

> Now Jesus went about all Galilee, teaching in their synagogues, preaching the gospel of the kingdom… (Matthew 4:23)

The gospel of the kingdom addresses activity within the body of Christ following Jesus' death on the cross. When we repent of our sins and accept Jesus Christ as our Savior, we enter the body of Christ.

> For by one Spirit we were all baptized into one body… and have all been made to drink into one Spirit… Now you are the body of Christ, and members individually. (1 Corinthians 12:13, 27)

Jesus often spoke in parables concerning the kingdom of heaven. The parables tell us in a figurative sense how we are to live while dwelling in the body of Christ. The kingdom of heaven is the body of Christ of which Jesus is the head. This entity is also referred to as the Church—a place where Christians grow and establish within themselves the mind of Christ.

At the end of this age, the kingdom will be handed to the Father.

> Then comes the end, when He delivers the kingdom to God the Father, when He puts an end to all rule and all authority and power. (1 Corinthians 15:24)

Jesus claimed to be the *Alpha* and the *Omega*, the Beginning and the End. The *Omega* involves handing the kingdom to the Father at the end, which coincides with the end of all rule, authority and power. The New Testament covers the introduction, implementation, and the conclusion of the kingdom of heaven, but the design and plan for the kingdom of heaven seems to be unaddressed. So where is the *Alpha*, the Beginning?

The beginning is mentioned in the first chapter of John:

> He was in the beginning with God. All things were made through Him, and without Him nothing was made that was made. (John 1:2, 3)

These verses reference Jesus, showing how He was quite involved in the creation process.

Following this train of thought, this statement draws us to the creation narrative in Genesis 1. If one were to look at the seven days of creation in a figurative or allegorical sense, perhaps the hidden message would show the outline for the kingdom of heaven. After all, it sets the foundation for all of Scripture, and given that the kingdom of heaven is the first major topic of our Lord's teaching in the New Testament, it could very well be the Alpha, or the beginning of His kingdom.

Scripture is no stranger to figurative prose. Just as Jesus spoke in parables during His ministry, similar symbolic language is applied elsewhere. When appearing in the book of Revelation, He speaks in symbols and types. With the appearance of Jesus in the creation process, it wouldn't be unusual for Him to speak in a figurative sense as well. Upon reading Genesis 1, there's a distinct possibility that the author is speaking figuratively, and there could be a hidden allegorical meaning behind the seven days of creation.

Treating the creation narrative as an allegory and interpreting the symbols and types can be quite challenging. This investigative process involves biblical hermeneutics, the art and science of interpreting the communication of God to man.

The first step of studying Scripture is to overcome one's resistance to presuming that beneath the surface of Scripture lies another meaning at a higher level. Scripture is often multi-layered, and beyond first glance, the interpretation simply requires an open mind.

Taking this into account, this does not dispel the fact that God created the heavens and the earth. However, while the creationists are battling against the evolutionists, they are ignoring the possibility of an allegorical interpretation of the creation narrative as well. Be that as it may, another hat is tossed into the ring.

This book, based on exegetical theology, intends to present a unique, theologically sound interpretation of each of the seven days of creation, which will in turn lead to a much greater in-depth understanding of the holy Scriptures—an understanding that will provide a refreshing wind to the churches. The book will engage readers in a spiritual archaeological digging, showing how the first five days of creation relate to the design and plan for the kingdom of heaven, how the sixth day refers to the implementation of the kingdom, and how the seventh day reveals the handing of the kingdom to the Father.

Introduction

In the early '90s, I had completed coursework in pursuit of a master of arts degree in biblical studies at the Mission Bay Christian Fellowship School of Ministries in San Diego, California. The final project for graduation involved writing a thesis. One Sunday evening, I was reading Luke 22. For some reason, the following two verses grabbed my attention:

> Then He said to them, "But now, he who has a money bag, let him take it, and likewise a sack; and he who has no sword, let him sell his garment and buy one"... Then they said, "Lord, look, here are two swords." And He said to them, "It is enough." (Luke 22:36, 38)

Having read this passage many times before, I wondered why I never took notice of verse 38—"Lord, look, here are two swords." Knowing that the Lord spoke in a figurative sense, I studied Jesus' reply, and came up with the conclusion that the two swords were *logos* and *rhema*.

These two words have similar Greek meanings. *Rhema* is "that which is spoken," and *logos* is "a word, a thing uttered." In the process of performing this study, I found that *logos* was associated with knowledge, and *rhema* was associated with understanding.

As one thing led to another, I further found a relationship between what was written in Genesis 1 and a statement made by the Lord in the book of Jeremiah:

> For My people are foolish, they have not known Me. They are silly children, and they have **no understanding**. They are wise to do evil, but to do good they have **no knowledge**. I beheld **the earth, and indeed it was without form, and void; and the heavens, they had no light**. (Jeremiah 4:22, 23)

Reading the reference to the origins of creation and how it relates to Jeremiah's prophecy, it was at this point that I began to examine the seven days of creation, as if there might be a hidden meaning behind it. What I had discovered in a short order of time was that the seven days of creation appeared to be an allegory pointing to the creation of a school—hence the reference to "understanding" and "knowledge"—in which the first five days are five elements that define the school structure.

Upon entering the body of Christ, the Lord wants His followers to establish within themselves the mind of Christ. This activity is made available in such places as church services, Sunday school classes, or perhaps small group meetings involving Bible studies. Christ's disciples need to be schooled. This was the purpose for designing and planning a school for those who enter the body of Christ, the kingdom of heaven.

With this in mind, I now had fodder for my thesis. It took almost a year to complete the 40,000-word thesis which was titled, *The Seven Days of Creation*. It basically pointed out that the first five days consisted of information in the form of knowledge and understanding, the school itself, students, instructors, and tests, and that the sixth day involved implementation of the school.

Given this unique concept of the deeper implications of creation, I decided to boil the thesis down into a book, which I published in 1996, also titled, *The Seven Days of Creation*. Following retirement, I spent time revising the book while traveling the West Coast for a couple of months. During this period, the book seemed to move in a different direction with a focus on the kingdom of heaven. Upon further study, I discovered a parallel to the "school" concept, only this time I discovered that the first five days of creation were the plan and design for the kingdom of heaven, that the sixth day was the implementation of the kingdom of heaven, and that the seventh day was when the kingdom was handed to the Father.

With this new twist, this updated version of the original book will provide a rather interesting interpretation of the creation narrative and reveal hidden spiritual meanings behind each day of creation. The reader will discover that the first five days of creation contain five spiritually discerned ingredients for the establishment of a school, and that this establishment is the design and plan for the kingdom of heaven. Each detail supports the premise that the kingdom of heaven is introduced and implemented following the birth of Christ, and that God will rest on the seventh day when the kingdom is handed to the Father at the end of the age.

This concept is the unveiling of a mystery that has been either hidden or lost since the Scriptures were written. Knowing this vital information, you can embrace a depth to the creation story that will impact your understanding of God and the future He has planned out for His creation.

Chapter 1

The First Day

Section I – The Purpose of Creation

In the beginning God created the heavens and the earth. (Genesis 1:1)

This creation included all things—both tangible and intangible.

You are worthy, O Lord, to receive glory and honor and power, for You created all things, and by Your will they exist and were created. (Revelation 5:8)

"All things" included mankind. But for what purpose? Luke offers an answer to this question in Acts chapter 17:

... He gives to all life, breath, and all things. And He has made from one blood every nation of men to dwell on all the face of the earth, and has determined their preappointed times and the boundaries of their habitation, **so that**

they should seek the Lord... (Acts 17:25–27; bolded for emphasis)

The purpose for mankind's existence is to seek God. Every nation of men includes the gentiles. A gentile is a person who is not a Jew.

After this I will return and will rebuild the tabernacle of David which has fallen down. I will rebuild its ruins, and I will set it up, **so that the rest of mankind may seek the Lord, even all the gentiles** who are called by My name, says the Lord who does all these things. (Acts 15:16, 17; bolded for emphasis)

Knowing that the purpose of life is to seek God, the question now becomes, "What does it mean to seek God?"

If then you were raised with Christ, **seek those things which are above**, where Christ is sitting at the right hand of God. Set your mind on things above, not on things on the earth. For you died, and your life is hidden with Christ in God. When Christ who is our life appears, then you also will appear with Him in glory. (Colossians 2:20)

The apostle John tells us that as children of God, we must purify ourselves.

Beloved, now we are children of God; and it has not yet been revealed what we shall be, but we know that when He is revealed, we shall be like Him, for we shall see Him as He is. And everyone who has this hope in Him purifies himself, just as He is pure. (1 John 3:2, 3)

If we are to become like Him—holy as our Father is holy—then we must move on to perfection. Yet perfection sounds so unattainable in the human experience. Scripture addresses this concept of human perfection in several passages.

Therefore, you shall be perfect, just as the Father in heaven is perfect. (Matthew 5:48)

Therefore, leaving the discussion of the elementary principles of Christ, let us go on to perfection... (Hebrews 6:1)

This does not mean that individuals will acquire the all-encompassing perfection of God. Paul comments on this in the following verses from his letter to the Philippians:

Not that I have already attained, or am already perfected; but I press on, that I may lay hold of that for which Christ Jesus has also laid hold of me. Brethren, I do not count myself to have apprehended; but one thing I do, forgetting those things which are behind and reaching forward to those things which are ahead. (Philippians 3:12, 13)

One must be careful when stating that we are to become like God, for Satan also claimed that he will be like the Most High. Such a boast led to his downfall. The following verses describe the five "I will" statements of Satan that led to his fall from heaven:

How you are fallen from heaven, O Lucifer, son of the morning! How you are cut down to the ground, you who weakened the nations! For you have said in your heart: "I will ascend into heaven, I will exalt my throne above the stars of God; I will also sit on the mount of the congregation on the farthest sides of the north; I will ascend above the heights of the clouds, **I will be like the Most High**." (Isaiah 14:12–14; bolded for emphasis)

Satan wanted God's position of authority, and he hungered for power. One must not be endangered with a philosophy that parallels Satan's pride—and thus his fall. In order to avoid the same mistake that Satan made, those who seek to be like God should limit themselves to attributes similar to the fruit of the Spirit.

But the fruit of the Spirit is love, joy, peace, longsuffering, kindness, goodness, faithfulness, gentleness, self-control... (Galatians 5:22, 23)

We should clothe ourselves in these attributes by demonstrating them in everyday life, and humble ourselves before the throne, rather than exalt ourselves to the throne.

Looking at it from another aspect, in his epistle to the Romans, Paul associates the attributes of God to the creation:

For since the creation of the world His invisible attributes are clearly seen, being understood by things that are made, even His eternal power and Godhead, so that they are without excuse. (Romans 1:20)

This verse stresses the importance of knowing God's character so that mankind will have no excuse when faced with the righteous judgment of God. If man knows that God values humility, love, and faithfulness, he is accountable to God to act accordingly. Since God intentionally created a world that demonstrates His attributes by things that He made, then it seems reasonable to assume that we are to seek these attributes and build our character around them.

Section II – Light versus Darkness

The earth was without form, and void; and darkness was on the face of the deep. And the Spirit of God was hovering over the face of the waters. (Genesis 1:2)

Darkness is concealment, obscurity, secrecy, deception, or the lack of knowledge or insight. The mention of darkness in the creation story serves to offset light. In His later description of the condition of His people during the time of Jeremiah the prophet, God equates a lack of knowledge and understanding of His ways to darkness:

For My people are foolish, they have not known Me. They are silly children, and they have **no understanding**. They are wise to do evil, but to do good they have **no knowledge**. I beheld **the earth, and indeed it was without form, and**

void; and the heavens, they had no light. (Jeremiah 4:22, 23; bolded for emphasis)

Notice the similarity between the words of the last sentence in the above quote and those mentioned in Genesis 1:2, which says, "The earth was without form, and void; and darkness was on the face of the deep. And the Spirit of God was hovering over the face of the waters."

In Genesis 1:2, water is mentioned twice—the "face of the deep" and the "face of the waters." Further examination by cross-referencing Scripture shows that the waters are symbolic of nations and peoples of the earth, a symbology also used in Revelation chapter 17.

And he (angel) said to me, "The waters which you saw, where the harlot sits, are peoples, multitudes, nations, and tongues." (Revelation 17:15)

The deep is the inward portion or heart of the waters. The Hebrew word for heart is *labab*, which in a general sense means "the midst, the innermost, or the hidden parts of things." It evokes a personal essence. The expression "darkness was upon the face of the deep" means that darkness was on the hearts of the people of the earth.

The apostle Paul describes the condition of the people at the time of Christ in his letter to the Roman Church:

... and their foolish hearts were darkened. (Romans 1:21)

Darkness was on the face of the deep. The outward manifestation of the condition of the heart of mankind was seen as the Holy Spirit hovered over the face of the waters, for God foreknew the hearts of men even at the time of creation. Paul goes on to describe this outward manifestation:

Therefore God also gave them up to uncleanness, in the lusts of their hearts, to dishonor their bodies among themselves, who exchange the truth for the lie, and worshiped and served the creature rather than the Creator, who is blessed forever. Amen. For this reason God gave them up to vile passions.

5

For even their women exchanged the natural use for what is against nature. Likewise also the men, leaving the natural use of their woman, burned in their lust one for another, men with men committing what is shameful, and receiving in themselves the penalty of their error which was due. And even as they did not like to retain God in their knowledge, God gave them over to a debased mind, to do those things which are not fitting; being filled with all unrighteousness, sexual immorality, wickedness, covetness, maliciousness; full of envy, murder, strife, deceit, evil-mindedness; they are whisperers, backbiters, haters of God, violent, proud, boasters, inventors of evil things, disobedient to parents, undiscerning, untrustworthy, unloving, unforgiving, unmerciful; (Romans 1:24–31)

Knowing the spiritual condition of His people ahead of time, God designed and planned the kingdom of heaven from the very beginning. He began by establishing light—which is true knowledge of His righteous ways.

Then God said, "Let there be light"; and there was light. And God saw the light, that it was good... (Genesis 1:3, 4)

In the beginning was the Word, and Word was with God, and Word was God. He was in the beginning with God. All things were made through Him, and without Him nothing was made that was made. In Him was life, and the life was the light of men. And the light shines in the darkness, and the darkness did not comprehend it. (John 1:1–5)

Only by living in the light of Christ can man begin to understand the kingdom of heaven and the implications that it brings.

Section III – Salvation and the Kingdom of Heaven

Given that our purpose in life is to seek God, He is good to help those who desire to do so. In the beginning, God designed and planned what was to be called the kingdom of heaven. This kingdom is like an educational facility where knowledge and understanding of His attributes are administered to disciples.

Christ's death on the cross gave everyone the opportunity to receive the gift of eternal life. Upon accepting that gift, we enter the kingdom of heaven. While in the kingdom of heaven, it is God's desire that we seek His attributes, grow in Him, develop within us the mind of Christ and encourage others to do the same.

The first day of creation, as addressed in Genesis 1, is the first of five ingredients that make up the kingdom of heaven. This foundational ingredient consists of knowledge and understanding of the ways of God. Knowledge and understanding of His attributes are provided in three primary ways—the written word, the Holy Spirit, and Christian ministry.

The written word comes to us through the Holy Bible. For the serious disciple, an excellent study Bible is recommended. Various Bible study guides, such as concordances, lexicons, expository dictionaries, and commentaries, are quite helpful in understanding the written word.

Accompanying our own human efforts, Jesus promised to send the Holy Spirit to teach us following His ascension:

> And I will pray the Father, and He will give you another Helper, that He may abide with you forever, even the Spirit of truth… But the Helper, the Holy Spirit, whom the Father will send in My name, He will teach you all things, and bring remembrance all things that I said to you… when He, the Spirit of truth, has come, He will guide you into all truth… (John 14:16, 17, 26; 16:13)

God also promised to send shepherds to teach knowledge and understanding of His ways:

> And I will give you shepherds according to My heart, who will feed you with **knowledge** and **understanding**. (Jeremiah 3:15; bolded for emphasis)

> And He Himself gave some to be apostles, some prophets, some evangelists, and some pastors and teachers, for the

equipping of the saints for the work of ministry, for the edifying of the body of Christ, till we all come to the unity of the faith and the knowledge of the Son of God, to a perfect man, to the measure of the stature of the fullness of Christ. (Ephesians 4:13)

The key words in these passages are "knowledge" and "understanding."

For the Lord gives wisdom; from His mouth come knowledge and understanding. (Proverbs 2:6)

Section IV – Knowledge, Understanding, and Wisdom

Knowledge is defined as an "awareness of facts." Knowledge of the ways of God is referred to as light.

For it is God who commanded light to shine out of darkness who has shone in our hearts to give the light of the knowledge of the glory of God in the face of Jesus Christ. (2 Corinthians 4:6)

Jesus clearly stated that He is the light of the world:

Then Jesus spoke to them again, saying, "I am the light of the world." (John 8:12)

This light consisted of not only knowledge of the ways of God, but also knowledge of the kingdom of heaven.

Now Jesus went about all Galilee, teaching in their synagogues, preaching the gospel of the kingdom... (Matthew 4:23)

Jesus is the light of life.

In Him was life, and the life was the light of men. (John 1:4)

Hence, if we follow each of these thoughts through, knowledge illuminates our minds, which occurs through knowing Jesus, and further gives us deeper understanding of the kingdom of heaven.

Understanding differs from knowledge in that it interprets facts in order to comprehend, to perceive, to discern, or to recognize. Properly interpreting the light is the key to opening the eyes of the blind. The source of understanding is the Holy Spirit.

> How that by revelation knowledge He made known to me the mystery… by which, when you read, you may understand my knowledge in the mystery of Christ, which in other ages was not made known to the sons of men, as it has now been revealed by the Spirit to His holy apostles and prophets. (Ephesians 3:3–5)

An example of the Holy Spirit providing understanding of the light was when John introduced John the Baptist. John 1:5 states:

> And the light shines in the darkness, and the darkness did not comprehend it.

Further in verses 6 and 7, John the Baptist comes along bearing witness of the light. He understood the light. What was different about John the Baptist that he was able to comprehend the light and the others couldn't?

> …He will also be filled with the Holy Spirit, even from his mother's womb. (Luke 1:15)

John the Baptist was filled with the Holy Spirit in order to identify and bear witness of the coming light of the world. When light arrived, the earth was no longer void of the attributes of God. Understanding is recognizing the truth in the midst of darkness.

> And God saw the light, that it was good; and God divided the light from the darkness. (Genesis 1:4)

God separated the light from the darkness in order for people to understand which attributes are associated with God and which are associated with evil.

...And the knowledge of the Holy One is understanding. (Proverbs 9:10)

With the ability to comprehend the light via the Holy Spirit, John was able to provide knowledge of the kingdom of heaven that was at hand.

Other examples that show the difference between knowledge and understanding are the parables of the sower and the wheat and tares recounted in Matthew 13. Jesus often speaks to the multitudes in parables. However, many listeners don't understand them. As explained in Chapter 13, Jesus interprets both of these parables for his disciples so that they could understand what He was saying.

Understanding is needed in order to retain sound doctrine (Matthew 16:9, 11), to recognize the enemy (Mark 13:14), to heal or to be healed (John 12:40), to comprehend the Scriptures (Luke 24:45), to clearly see God's attributes through things that are made (Romans 1:20), and to discern between that which is good and that which is evil (1 Kings 3:9).

Wisdom can be defined as "knowledge applied." It is the ability to take knowledge and apply it to all life's opportunities, challenges, and circumstances. The relationship of knowledge, understanding, and wisdom is shown in the following table:

	Definition
Knowledge	Possession of facts
Understanding	Interpretation of facts
Wisdom	Application of facts

Section V – The Two Swords

The gospel of the kingdom contains the light that illuminates the way we are to live. The Holy Spirit will remind us of what is of the light and provide the understanding that separates the light from darkness. During the Passover meal, or what is commonly known as The Last Supper, Jesus mentioned the importance of being filled with the Holy Spirit. The Holy Spirit allows believers deeper insight into the Scriptures. During this same conversation, Jesus spoke to those around Him and made reference to buying a sword. The Holy Spirit allows us to dissect this verse to find the significance of the sword, and how it relates to the kingdom.

> Then He said to them, "But now, he who has a money bag, let him take it, and likewise a sack, and he who has no sword, let him sell his garment and buy one." (Luke 22:36)

Take careful note of the wording here. In verse 36, the disciple is not to use the money in the money bag to buy a sword, but the disciple is told to sell his garment to buy a sword. A couple of verses later, *two* swords are mentioned.

> Then they said, "Lord, look, here are two swords." And He said to them, "It is enough." (Luke 22:38)

The resounding question is, "What are the two swords?" Also, what did Jesus mean when he said, "Buy a sword"? A literal interpretation of the text might imply a physical sword, but further scrutiny shows something different.

What could a group of followers do with two swords against the Roman army? In reading just a few verses further, Peter cuts of the ear of the servant of the high priest when they came to arrest Jesus. Those with Jesus said, "Shall we strike with the sword?" Jesus implies, "No! That is not what I meant when I said to purchase a sword," as He heals the servant's ear.

We know that Jesus quite often spoke in a figurative sense. He taught in parables and made spiritual applications of physical things. The answer as to the spiritual meaning of the sword mentioned in Luke 22:36 seems to lie in Ephesians 6.

> Finally, my brethren, be strong in the Lord and in the power of His might. Put on the whole armor of God, that you may

11

be able to stand against the wiles of the devil. For we do not wrestle against flesh and blood, but against principalities, against powers, against the rulers of the darkness of this age, against spiritual hosts of wickedness in the heavenly places. Therefore, take up the whole armor of God, that you may be able to withstand in the evil day, and having done all, to stand. Stand therefore, having girded your waist with truth, having put on the breastplate of righteousness, and having shod your feet with the preparation of the gospel of peace; above all, taking the shield of faith with which you will be able to quench all the fiery darts of the wicked one. And take the helmet of salvation, and the **sword of the Spirit, which is the word of God**; (Ephesians 6:10–17; bolded for emphasis)

According to Luke 22:36, we are to sell our worldly garment. In Ephesians 6, we are to replace it with the armor of God. Remember, Jesus did not say to use the money in the money bag to buy a sword. He said to sell your garment and buy a sword.

The Greek translation of *word* in Ephesians 6:17 is *rhema*. *Rhema* means "that which is spoken." Since it's the sword of the Spirit, the sword is therefore "that which is spoken by the Spirit."

What could the other sword be? Another Greek word that is translated as "word" in English has a similar meaning to *rhema*, which means "a thing uttered or expressed in words." That word is *logos*.

Because this interpretation is very similar to *rhema*, both *logos* and *rhema* are interpreted in English as one word—that is, *word*. One would surmise that if they held the same meaning in Greek, then there would not have been two different words used. It seems to make sense that there is a slight difference, or perhaps a big difference, in the meaning of those words.

To discover the Bible's intention here, let's go to John 1.

In the beginning was the Word, and the Word was with God, and the Word was God. (John 1:1)

The Greek word used here is *logos*, and it is used again a few verses later.

> And the Word became flesh and dwelt among us, and we beheld His glory, the glory as of the only begotten of the Father, full of grace and truth. (John 1:14)

Who is John speaking of here? We know that the Word that became flesh is Jesus. The Greek word for Jesus is YHSOUS, which means Savior. "The only begotten of the Father" implies that He is the Son of God. The two swords are *logos* and *rhema*. *Logos* is associated with Jesus the Savior, and *rhema* is associated with the Holy Spirit.

From reading the gospel of John, we know that Jesus is the *logos*, the light of the world, the way, the truth, and the life. John the Baptist aptly demonstrated this as he was able to understand the light because he was filled with the Holy Spirit.

One sword was *logos*—Jesus, life, and light. This sword was used to pierce the darkness of our souls. The second sword separates the light from the darkness. It was the understanding of God. Understanding comes from the heart.

> He has blinded their eyes and hardened their heart, lest they should see with their eyes and understand with their heart. (John 12:40)

> Having their understanding darkened... because of the hardening of the heart... (Ephesians 4:18)

In John 2, at the wedding in Cana, the Lord begins His ministry. At this event He turns water into wine. Through this demonstration, He is announcing a new message which is better than the old message. Whether it's old or new, the wine represented knowledge or truth concerning God and His way of living. Given that Jesus was the Christ, or the anointed Savior, He had the anointing oil of the Holy Spirit. Thus, He possessed not just knowledge, but understanding as well.

The significance behind oil—Christ's anointing oil—and wine sheds new meaning to the third seal (scarcity on the earth) mentioned in Revelation 6:

> Do not harm the oil and the wine [understanding and knowledge of His ways]. (Revelation 6:6)

Words associated with the two swords can be summarized in the following table:

Sword 1	Logos, Jesus, Savior, light, way, truth, life, wine, knowledge
Sword 2	Rhema, Holy Spirit, truth, heart, oil, understanding

Note: The common word to each sword is "truth."

Returning to Luke 22, the sword of Jesus was the *logos* of God. It was shining before John the Baptist was born, it was shining at the time of the Last Supper, and it continues to shine today. The word "shines" in John 1:5 means that the light was always shining and continues to shine. This same sword does not need to be purchased. That is why Jesus said to purchase only one sword—the ever-shining sword of the Spirit.

The sword of the Spirit arrived with John the Baptist. Until the death of John the Baptist, with the exception of the twelve that were anointed and sent out in Matthew 10 and Mark 6, John and Jesus were the only two main characters wielding the sword of the Spirit. Remember, in verse 36, the Lord said, "And he who has no sword," which implies that some of those in the group possessed the sword of the Spirit and others did not. With the possible exception of the twelve apostles being filled with the Spirit, after the ascension of Jesus, the sword of the Spirit departed, leaving only the sword of *logos*.

In essence, Jesus was telling those at the Last Supper that when He departs, the Holy Spirit is departing with Him, and that He wanted those who weren't already filled with the Spirit to be filled with the Spirit. Jesus told His disciples to tarry in Jerusalem. Why? Acts 2 gives us the answer—Jesus wanted them to await Pentecost, when the Holy Spirit descended on believers.

During the first day of creation, light (knowledge) and separation of light from darkness (understanding) is being introduced as part of the design and plan for the kingdom of heaven, and by association, one could surmise that knowledge (light) represents the activity of Jesus. That understanding (separation of light from darkness) represents the activity of the Holy Spirit. Obviously, when Jesus became filled with the Holy Spirit after His baptism in the Jordan River, He functioned with both knowledge and understanding.

Section VI – The Fall of Man

In the Garden of Eden, life was pleasant for Adam and Eve until Satan, the prince of darkness, arrives on the scene. He convinces Eve to disobey God.

> But of the fruit of the tree which is in the midst of the garden, God has said, "You shall not eat it, nor shall you touch it, lest you die." And the serpent said to the woman, "You will not surely die."… So when the woman saw that the tree was good for food, that it was pleasant to the eyes, and a tree desirable to make one wise, she took of its fruit and ate… (Genesis 3:3, 4, 6)

In the beginning, Adam and Eve knew God's true way of living, and they lived according to this truth. Then Eve exchanged the truth for a lie. As a result of this sin, man was driven from the garden. This one deception was enough to cause great wickedness on the earth. When mankind was left in the hands of Satan, knowledge of God's character became void on the earth. Truth was rejected, and mankind lived according to his own thoughts. The earth became void of God's true way of living. God answered this wickedness with a great flood. As Paul explains,

> because, although they knew God, they did not glorify Him as God, nor were thankful, but became futile in their thoughts, and…**who exchanged the truth of God for the lie…** (Romans 1:21, 25)

Before Eve's choice, in the Garden of Eden Adam and Eve lived in peace and walked with God. After disobedience, they were forced out of Eden, and the way to the tree of life in the Garden of Eden was blocked by cherubim and a flaming sword that turned in every direction.

This was the beginning of the fall of man. It was also the beginning of the road to recovery—the redemption of mankind.

Section VII – Elohim

The plural use of God in the first three chapters of Genesis has puzzled many readers. In general, theologians refer to this plurality as being the triune God consisting of the Father, Son and Holy Spirit.

The Hebrew word for God used in these passages is *elohim*. It is the plural form of *eloahh,* which means "a deity or God." In the beginning, the triune God created things in order to demonstrate the Father's attributes. Creation is centered on providing mankind an opportunity to perfect itself with God's character. The Father orchestrates the whole scheme of things through the use of the Son and the Holy Spirit. Thus the three parts work together for the good of the whole.

As each part of the trinity has a role, Scripture focuses on revealing the knowledge of God as demonstrated by Jesus, the light of the world. This light (logos), an expression of God, is interpreted through the Holy Spirit. Once again, all three units of the *elohim* work together to bring about the salvation message.

> Casting down arguments and every high thing that exalts itself against the knowledge of God, bringing every thought into captivity to the obedience of Christ, (2 Corinthians 10:5)

Section VIII – At Day's End

The earth was void of knowledge and was without form (no understanding). For darkness was on the face of the deep (the hearts of mankind). The arrival of light provided knowledge and understanding of the way we should live. This light has been shining from the beginning, and it continues to shine.

A river of truth runs through Scripture. It is a river that contains knowledge and understanding of the ways of God. This river analogy holds incredible significance, for it has its beginning in Genesis and flows between the wings of the two cherubim in the Holy of Holies in the tabernacle of Moses.

> And there I will meet with you, and I will speak with you from above the mercy seat, from between the two cherubim... (Exodus 25:22)

And the "speaker" sheds understanding:

> For the Lord gives wisdom; from His mouth come knowledge and understanding. (Proverbs 2:6)

The river can be seen flowing between the two olive trees mentioned in Zechariah, the two swords mentioned in Luke, and then finally between the last two witnesses called out in the book of Revelation. What does this river theme share among each of these analogies?

The river carries truth. And truth is founded on knowledge and understanding.

Knowledge and understanding provide us with the way we are to live as God's chosen people. Combined, they are the first of five ingredients for establishing the kingdom of heaven, a place where man has the opportunity to be molded into the image of God. Growing in Him enhances the glory of God. As you dwell in the kingdom of heaven, do not be complacent. Continue to seek after God's attributes and apply them to your life so that you might be in the light, not the darkness.

After God separated light from darkness, He gave names to light and darkness:

> God called the light Day, and the darkness He called Night. So the evening and the morning were the first day. (Genesis. 1:5)

The first six days end with the expression "the evening and the morning were the... day." The evening is the time when light is replaced by darkness. The morning is the time when darkness is overcome by light. Each of the first six days is concerned with various aspects of man's progression as he struggles in an arena of truth and error as typified by light and darkness.

Chapter 2

The Second Day

Section I – The Firmament

As children of God, we are expected to live according to His way of living. In His goodness, God provided the knowledge and understanding necessary to guide us. This was addressed in the first day of creation. The second day of creation provides a place, or school, where a person may obtain this knowledge.

> Then God said, "Let there be a firmament in the midst of the waters, and let it divide the waters from the waters." Thus God made the firmament, and divided the waters which were under the firmament from the waters which were above the firmament; and it was so. And God called the firmament Heaven. So the evening and the morning were the second day. (Genesis 1:6–8)

Two waters are identified in this passage. One reference to water was mentioned earlier in our study as being peoples, multitudes, nations, and tongues of the earth (Revelation 17:15). These were the waters that were *under* the firmament. The other water symbolism is associated with the kingdom of God.

> And he showed me a pure river of water of life, clear as crystal, proceeding from the throne of God and of the Lamb. (Revelation 22:1)

People of the nations of the world who sincerely seek after God will have the opportunity to drink of the river of eternal life. In order to drink of the river of life, one needs to cross the firmament that was placed between the two waters.

The firmament, or heaven as God named it, is a realm that bridges the gap between the kingdom of God and the kingdom of the earth. This bridge is depicted by some Christians as a cross in which the bottom rests on the planet earth and the top rests in the spiritual kingdom of the Father.

The condition of the world was such that God would not allow people to have free access to His kingdom. They were a people of darkness.

> For all have sinned and fall short of the glory of God. (Romans 3:23)

Therefore, God separated the world from His kingdom. However, in order to fulfill His promise of eternal life to those who turned to Him, God provided a way by which they may enter His kingdom. This way is a heaven that allows those who elect Christ as their Savior to cross over into the Father's kingdom.

Heaven in Greek *ouranos* means "that which embraces all things in the absolute." It encompasses all conceivable life within its bounds. A study on how the word was used in various writings near the time of Christ indicates that heaven is used to define one of three states: natural, metaphysical and spiritual.

Natural relates to the earth, while spiritual relates to an incorporeal existence. Metaphysical combines the two in a mixture of natural and spiritual entities.

The New Testament opens with John the Baptist and Jesus Christ proclaiming the kingdom of heaven—signifying this metaphysical realm.

> In those days John the Baptist came preaching in the wilderness of Judea, and saying, "Repent, for the kingdom of heaven is at hand!" (Matthew 3:1, 2)

> From that time Jesus began to preach and to say, "Repent, for the kingdom of heaven is at hand." (Matthew 4:17)

The expression "the kingdom of heaven" is found over thirty times in Matthew's gospel, and it refers to one kingdom, not two or more kingdoms. There are two significant kingdoms mentioned in Scripture: the kingdom of the Son and the kingdom of the Father. The distinction between the Son's kingdom and the Father's kingdom is mentioned in Matthew 13.

> The Son of Man will send out His angels, and they will gather out of His kingdom all things that offend, and those who practice lawlessness... then the righteous will shine forth as the sun in the kingdom of their Father. (Matthew 13:41, 43)

The concept that Christ's kingdom is separate from the Father's kingdom is reinforced in the following verse:

> For He must reign till He has put all enemies under His feet. Then comes the end, when He delivers the kingdom to God the Father, when He puts an end to all rule and all authority and power. (1 Corinthians 15:24, 25)

The kingdom of the Son is not of this earth. Jesus emphasized this in response to Pilate's questioning.

> Jesus answered, "My kingdom is not of this world. If My kingdom were of this world, My servants would fight, so that I should not be delivered to the Jews; but now My kingdom is not from here." (John 18:36)

However, His kingdom does include people of the earth. As mentioned in Matthew 13, Jesus will send forth His angels and cast out of His kingdom those who practice lawlessness. Those who repent of their sins and accept Jesus as their Savior will enter the body of Christ, the kingdom of heaven. In order for Christ's kingdom to not be of the world, yet contain people of the world, it would have to be metaphysical in essence—both natural and spiritual.

Jesus Christ wants His disciples to achieve perfection, something only the spiritual can provide a way to. The Son's kingdom is the sphere of activity where Christians grow in the Lord. What we know of the Father is through the Son. What is presented through Christ in the Son's kingdom is what we know of the Father's kingdom. The kingdom of heaven is a type of the Father's kingdom, and its characteristics are a subset of the Father's kingdom. The Son's kingdom is a place where one grows in the Lord, much like a mustard seed.

The remaining books of the New Testament following the gospel of Matthew use the expression "kingdom of God" instead of "kingdom of heaven." For example, Mark uses the expression "kingdom of God" in the following verse, which is parallel to what Matthew mentions several times as "the kingdom of heaven":

And saying, "The time is fulfilled, and the kingdom of God is at hand. Repent, and believe in the gospel." (Mark 1:15)

Another example of this slightly different language is found when Jesus commented on why He spoke in parables. In Matthew He references the "kingdom of heaven," but in Mark and Luke He references "the kingdom of God." Matthew helps make it easy for us to discern between the two kingdoms, since the variation in wording holds great significance. In general, in the book of Matthew, the kingdom of heaven refers to the Son's kingdom, while the kingdom of God refers to the Father's kingdom.

Section II – Parables Concerning the Kingdom of Heaven

Since God desires that we seek Him, be part of His kingdom, and become like Him, it is reasonable to assume that He would provide that which is needed to achieve these goals. His perfect character is found in the vast depth of His multi-dimensional nature. The attributes of this nature are made available in the kingdom of heaven.

The kingdom of heaven is a sphere of activity in which man seeks after God's righteousness. This truth is depicted in the many parables referencing the kingdom of heaven. Jesus revealed mysteries concerning the kingdom of heaven to His apostles and hid these same mysteries from the multitudes by speaking to them in parables.

> And the disciples came and said to Him, "Why do You speak to them in parables?" He answered and said to them, "Because it has been given to you to know the mysteries of the kingdom of heaven, but to them it has not been given." (Matthew 13:10, 11)

The parables indicate the various activities that take place in the kingdom of heaven. The Lord is good to explain the meaning of the first two parables concerning the kingdom of heaven—the parables of the sower and the wheat and tares. The interpretation of the parable of the sower is as follows:

> When anyone hears the word of the kingdom, and does not understand it, then the wicked one comes and snatches away what was sown in his heart. This is he who received seed by the wayside. But he who received the seed on stony places, this is he who hears the word and immediately receives it with joy; yet he has no root in himself, but endures only for a while. For when tribulation or persecution arises because of the word, immediately he stumbles. Now he who received seed among the thorns is he who hears the word, and the cares of this world and the deceitfulness of riches choke the word, and he becomes unfruitful. But he who received seed on the good ground is he who hears the word and

understands it, who indeed bears fruit and produces... (Matthew 13:19–23)

There are two activities going on in the parable of the sower. First, someone is sharing the gospel, and secondly, the word is received differently among the hearers of the word.

In the parable of the wheat and tares, the Lord breaks down the symbology and gives us a feel for interpreting His parables, aside from the fact that He said that we are not the ones to destroy the wicked, but He will take care of that at the end of the age.

The rest of the parables are left for us to interpret for ourselves. The parable of the mustard seed, for example, seems to refer to the word or gospel that is sown in the heart, and as we develop within us the mind of Christ, we grow from being babes to mature adult Christians.

> ... The kingdom of heaven is like a mustard seed, which a man took and sowed in his field, which indeed is the least of all the seeds; but when it is grown it is greater than the herbs and becomes a tree... (Matthew 13:31, 32)

Another of Jesus' illustrations, the parable of the leaven, is where knowledge and understanding of the ways of God increase over time and cause us to grow in Christ.

> ... The kingdom of heaven is like leaven, which a woman took and hid in three measures of meal till it was all leavened. (Matthew 13:33)

The next parable is a bit more difficult to interpret, as it mentions more abstract prose:

> Again, the kingdom of heaven is like treasure hidden in a field, which a man found and hid; and for joy over it he goes and sells all that he has and buys that field. (Matthew 13:44)

For this parable, we can use the explanation of the parable of the sower to help us. The treasure is something of great value: it is the word of the kingdom. The man hides the word in his heart. Unlike the person who received the word by the wayside, this man does not want the wicked one to snatch away what was sown in his heart. So, he puts aside the ways of the world and decides to follow Christ. He buys into a new way of life, the gospel of Jesus Christ.

> And do not be conformed to this world, but be transformed by the renewing of the mind, that you may prove what is that good and acceptable and perfect will of God. (Romans 12:2)

The parable of the pearl of great price shares a similar theme with the hidden treasure parable.

> Again, the kingdom of heaven is like a merchant seeking beautiful pearls, who, when he had found one pearl of great price, went and sold all that he had and bought it. (Matthew 13:45, 46)

The one pearl of great price is the gospel of Jesus Christ. The merchant sells his old way of life and purchases a new way of living.

In other examples of Jesus' teachings, the parable of the dragnet demonstrates commonalities with the parable of the wheat and tares in that angels will separate the wicked from among the just.

> Again, the kingdom of heaven is like a dragnet that was cast into the sea and gathered some of every kind, which when it was full, they drew it to shore; and they sat down and gathered the good into vessels, but threw the bad away. (Matthew 13:47, 48)

The parables focus on acquiring a new way of living based on the gospel of Jesus Christ, and when entering the kingdom of heaven, we are to grow as a mustard seed—ever maturing in Christ.

Section III – Types of the Kingdom of Heaven

The Tabernacle of Moses

The tabernacle of Moses depicted a shadow of things to come. It was a type of the kingdom of heaven, the body of Christ.

> Jesus answered and said to them, "Destroy this temple, and in three days I will raise it up... But He was speaking of His body. (John 2:19, 21)

The tabernacle of Moses was divided into three sections: the outer court, the inner court or Holy Place, and the Holy of Holies. Entrance to the tabernacle represents Jesus, or the one way by which we may enter into the kingdom of heaven.

> I am the door. If anyone enters by Me, he will be saved... (John 10:9)

There were two items in the outer court: the brazen altar and the brazen laver. The brazen altar in the outer court points to the ultimate sacrifice of Jesus Christ. Priests used the brazen laver to wash their hands and feet before entering the inner court, thus the laver represents cleansing ourselves in the word of God daily.

> That He might sanctify and cleanse it with the washing of water by the word. (Ephesians 5:26)

Moving inward within the tabernacle, there were three primary items in the inner court: the table of showbread, the golden candlestick, and the altar of incense. The golden candlestick had seven lamps and was the only light in the inner court. Although much could be said of this artifact, basically the lampstand represents Jesus as the light of the world. The seven lamps represent the sevenfold Spirit.

> ... And there were seven lamps of fire burning before the throne, which are the seven Spirits of God. (Revelation 4:5)

The sevenfold Spirit is described in Isaiah 11:

There shall come forth a Rod from the stem of Jesse, and a Branch shall grow out of his roots. The Spirit of the Lord shall rest upon Him, the Spirit of Wisdom and understanding, the Spirit of counsel and might, the Spirit of knowledge and of the fear of the Lord... But with righteousness He shall judge the poor. (Isaiah 11:1–4)

The twelve loaves of bread upon the table of showbread represent the spiritual food of the apostolic ministry. Jesus is the bread of life. Since we are a part of the body of Christ, we are the bread of life.

For we being many, are one bread and one body; for we all partake of that one bread. (1 Corinthians 10:17)

The wine at the table represents the blood shed for our sins. Eternal life depends on us drinking this wine and eating the bread.

Whoever eats My flesh and drinks My blood has eternal life... (John 6:54)

The altar of incense speaks of what we have to offer up to the Lord, such as our responsibilities to God. It includes our lifestyle that we present to the Lord as a sacrifice. It is at this altar where we offer up prayer, praise, intercession and worship. When people lift up their hands before the Lord in praise during worship, can they look back over the past week, examine their actions, and feel comfortable in offering their choices as a sweet fragrance to the Lord?

In Leviticus God defined for Moses the type of incense to be burned at this altar. Any other incense was unacceptable, much like God desires only offerings from us that honor Him.

Then Nadab and Abihu, the sons of Aaron, each took his censer and put fire in it, put incense on it, and offered profane fire before the Lord, which He had not commanded them. So fire went out from the Lord and devoured them, and they died before the Lord. Then Moses said to Aaron, "This is what the Lord spoke, saying: 'By those who come near Me I must be regarded as holy; And before all the people I must be glorified…'" (Leviticus 10: 1–3)

Lastly, within the Holy of Holies is a relic that many have sought after—the ark of the covenant. The ark was a large, ornate box decorated with two angels (cherubim) perched on each end, with a golden mercy seat between them. The ark had a chest that contained manna, Aaron's rod that budded, and the tables of law. Manna speaks of Jesus who is the bread of life. Aaron's rod that budded speaks of life after death. The tables of law lead us to Christ. The mercy seat in the ark implies the righteous judgment of Christ. The two cherubim represent knowledge and understanding of the ways of God. It is here where the Lord will speak between the wings of the cherubim.

> And there I will meet with you, and I will speak with you from above the mercy seat, from between the two cherubim… (Exodus 25:22)

Christians, being members of the body of Christ, have access to the Holy of Holies, because Jesus is our high priest and the high priest had direct access to the Holy of Holies. This position of Christ as high priest was signified when the veil that hid the Holy of Holies from the public was torn in two from top to bottom at the time of the crucifixion. With this great final act, the Lord wants us to dwell in the Holy of Holies. However, some insist on staying in the outer court. Others will go no further than the Holy Place. Blessed are those who go all the way to the Holy of Holies. As mentioned in the parable of the sower:

> But others fell on good ground and yielded a crop: some a hundredfold, some sixty, some thirty. (Matthew 13:8)

We must be hundredfold Christians.

The Tabernacle of David

Following a battle in which Israel was defeated by the Philistines, the Philistines captured the ark of the covenant. In preparation of the recovery and return of the ark, David pitched a tent for it in what was named the city of David, or Zion. Zion was a city within the city of Jerusalem. Upon its return, the ark was to be placed in the tent, and it was there that David celebrated before the Lord with dance, food, and music. (See 1 Chronicles 10–16.) The tent and the ark within is referred to as the Tabernacle of David. All this was taking place while regular worship was going on in the tabernacle of the Lord at Gibeon.

Today, as a result of the veil being torn following the crucifixion of Jesus Christ, we have access to the Holy of Holies, which contains the spiritual ark of the covenant. There we can dance and worship before the Lord our God as David did before the physical ark in Zion. The tabernacle of David is being restored.

There are two references to the tabernacle of David.

On that day I will raise up the tabernacle of David, which has fallen down, and repair its damages; I will raise up it ruins, and rebuild it as in the days of old. (Amos 9:11)

After this I will return and will rebuild the tabernacle of David which has fallen down. I will rebuild its ruins, and I will set it up, so that the rest of mankind may seek the Lord, even all the Gentiles who are called by My name, says the Lord who does all these things. (Acts 15:16, 17)

These verses speak of the restoration of the Church, the building up of a glorious habitation for the Spirit of God, to bring a harvest of souls to Christ.

Canaan

Canaan was the land of milk and honey. It was the promised land that God gave to his chosen people. The Jews wandered in the wilderness for forty years before going in and taking the land. In general, if the Jews obeyed the commands of God, they lived in relative peace in Canaan. When they disobeyed God, their enemies threatened, attacked, and even took them into captivity. Canaan was another type of the kingdom of heaven.

Adam and Eve were cast out of the Garden of Eden because of disobedience. Canaan was a place where mankind—God's chosen people—had to deal with the spirit of disobedience. It was a major step in the return to Eden.

The Body of Christ

When we decide to follow Jesus, we enter His body.

> For by one Spirit we were all baptized into one body...whether Jews or Greeks, whether slaves or free... and have all been made to drink into one Spirit. (1 Corinthians 12:13)

If a person enters the body of Christ, that person enters the kingdom of heaven. The head of the body is Christ.

> And He is the head of the body, the church.... (Colossians 1:18)

In the early Church, the disciples belonged to a group of Christian converts called "the Way."

> Then Saul, still breathing threats and murder against the disciples of the Lord, went to the high priest and asked letters from him to the synagogues of Damascus, so that if he found any who were of the Way, whether men or women, he might bring them bound to Jerusalem. (Acts 9:1, 2)

The Way existed in the kingdom of heaven through the body of Christ. The name of the group signified how one must travel the "way" through the kingdom of heaven in order to enter the Father's kingdom.

> Jesus said to him, "I am the way, the truth, and the life. No one comes to the Father except through Me." (John 14:6)

The key to this verse: Jesus is the true way to eternal life.

Section IV – The Name of Jesus

Jesus in Greek means "Savior." This is a fitting name, as it is through Him that we receive salvation.

And you shall call His name Jesus, for He will save His people from their sins. (Matthew 1:21)

Three aspects deal with our salvation. The firmament, the kingdom of heaven, and the body of Christ can all be considered as the way to salvation.

By searching a little deeper into the significance of Scripture, one can find all sorts of amazing clues as to how the details tie together. For example, using the Greek ciphered number system, the number that represents the name "Jesus" is 888.

	1	2	3	4	5	6	7	8	9
1	A	B	Γ	Δ	E	F	Z	H	Θ
10	I	K	Λ	M	N	Ξ	O	Π	Q
100	P	Σ	T	Y	Φ	X	Ψ	Ω	S

I	=	10
H	=	8
Σ	=	200
O	=	70
Y	=	400
Σ	=	200
	Total	888

It is interesting to note that Jesus was the Son of David, who was the eighth son of Jesse. The number eight is associated with salvation. This reasoning is supported in part by the salvation of Noah and his family during the great flood, for eight people (Noah, his wife, his three sons, and his sons' wives) were saved aboard the ark.

... God waited in the days of Noah, while the ark was being prepared, in which a few, that is, eight souls, were saved through water. (1 Peter 3:20)

The ark was symbolic of the kingdom of heaven. Those who did not enter the ark drowned in the sea of nations, or the ways of the world. The ark was a place of salvation. The story of Noah demonstrates the relationship between righteousness and salvation. This relationship is brought to light in 2 Peter.

And did not spare the ancient world, but saved Noah, one of **eight people**, a preacher of **righteousness**, bringing in the flood on the world of the ungodly. (2 Peter 2:5; bolded for emphasis)

Eight is commonly known as the number of "a new beginning." On the day of our salvation, we shall experience a new beginning.

The period of time from Adam to Christ was about four thousand years. From the time of Christ to the beginning of the thousand year reign is about two thousand years. In Revelation 20, Satan is cast into the bottomless pit and held there for one thousand years. During this time, those who had given their lives to Christ will reign with Him.

Blessed and holy is he who has part in the first resurrection. Over such the second death has no power, but they shall be priests of God and of Christ, and shall reign with Him a thousand years. (Revelation 20:6)

From the time of Adam, there are seven thousand years before entering the gates of New Jerusalem and eating of the tree of life. In Revelation 21, New Jerusalem comes down out of heaven from God. In Revelation 22, those who elected to follow Christ are allowed to enter the city and eat of the tree of eternal life. This is granted after the thousand year reign.

Blessed are those who do His commandments, that they may have the right to the tree of life, and may enter through the gates into the city. (Revelation 22:14)

In the following verse, the Bible assists the reader in the area of eschatological—or end times theology—interpretation by stating the interchange of one day and a thousand years.

> But the heavens and the earth which now exist are kept in store by the same word, reserved for fire until the day of judgment and perdition of ungodly men. But, beloved, do not forget this one thing, that with the Lord one day is as a thousand years, and a thousand years as one day. (2 Peter 3:7, 8)

The time of entering New Jerusalem is on the eighth day, for that is the day of new beginnings for those who have entered the Father's kingdom. This is also the time when Jesus hands His kingdom to the Father.

The Sabbath day of rest occurred on Saturday, the seventh day of the week. Jesus arose on the day following the Sabbath, the eighth day. When Jesus arose on Sunday—the day of His resurrection—Sunday became a new beginning for Christ. A passage from an extra-biblical writing[1] makes an interesting statement on this issue:

> "When resting from all things I shall begin the eighth day, that is, the beginning of the other world. For which cause we observe the eighth day with gladness, in which Jesus rose from the dead."

It's obvious that the day following the Sabbath is Sunday. It is the first day of a new week. The new week symbolically represent the new world or the Father's kingdom. Eight represents salvation. The first day of the new week is the day we enter the kingdom of God, our place of salvation. The eighth day is the day that follows the old week, and is the first day of the new week.

It's fitting for those who are part of the body of Christ to celebrate and worship on this day. Those who are free in Christ should elect to worship in unity and spirit on Sunday in honor of

---

1   *The Lost Books of The Bible and the Forgotten Books of Eden*, World Bible Publishers, Inc., 1926, Page 161.

Christ. Commemorating Christ's new beginning, along with our own, sets us apart from the rest of the world.

> But you are a chosen generation, a royal priesthood, a holy nation, His own special people, that you may proclaim the praises of Him who called you out of darkness into His marvelous light. (1 Peter 2:9)

The King James Version translates "special people" as "peculiar people." We are a peculiar people, obviously different from the rest of the world. Such differences include how we live out each day. Sunday is not a day of rest; it is a day of celebration. Saturday is the day of rest, and it should be honored as a day of rest. The Ten Commandments allocated this day as such:

> But the seventh day is the Sabbath of the Lord your God. In it you shall not do any work... (Deuteronomy 5:14)

Section V – A River Runs through It

Moses' tabernacle, Canaan, David's tabernacle, the body of Christ, and the kingdom of heaven each represent different aspects of the firmament that divides earthly man from the Father's kingdom. Together they make up the schoolhouse where we reside when we accept Christ as our Savior.

The Father sent His Son for the purpose of redeeming His lost creation and providing a way to eternal life. This purpose was facilitated by establishing the kingdom of heaven. The sins of the world could only be destroyed through the Son. A disciple having entered the kingdom of heaven through the body of Jesus Christ has entered into the truth and wisdom of Christ. We were predestined from the beginning to embrace the opportunity to enter the kingdom of heaven in order to receive salvation and redemption rather than to fall into the foolish ways of the world.

The intention of the kingdom of heaven was symbolically portrayed long ago by Jesus' death on the cross. The law was not adequate enough to destroy sin. In its own inadequacy, it attempted to destroy the one person that could destroy sin: Jesus. Through His death and resurrection, Christ took upon Himself the sins of the world and thus fulfilled the law's demands.

> Who Himself bore our sins in His own body on the tree, that we, having died to sins, might live for righteousness... (1 Peter 2:24)

If we enter the body of Christ, He forgives us of our sins and bears them in His own body. His body suffers from the burden of our sins. As the disciple matures in Christ, this burden is lifted. When a disciple suffers a relapse and sins again in an area that was cleansed, the disciple crucifies again the body of Christ.

> For it is impossible for those who...if they fall away, to renew again to repentance, since they crucify again for themselves the Son of God, and put Him to an open shame. (Hebrews 6:4–6)

Section VI – At Day's End

The second day describes the creation of a heaven—a place of learning—as part of the design and plan for the kingdom of heaven, a heaven later to be implemented following the ascension of our Lord Jesus Christ. It is the second of the five foundational elements for establishing a school that provides us with the opportunity to be molded into the image of God.

And so ends the second day concerning that which is good and that which is evil.

> So the evening and the morning were the second day. (Genesis 1:8)

Chapter 3

The Third Day

Section I – Disciples

God's Chosen People

At this point, we have knowledge and understanding of the way in which we are to live as Christians and a "schoolhouse" where this information is made available. But what good is this information and place of learning if there are no disciples (students)? Since the school is the kingdom of heaven, it makes sense that the door to the school was opened following the ascension of our Lord Jesus Christ. Now it's time to walk through that door. The third day of creation provides an environment that prepares students to enter the kingdom of heaven.

Prior to the birth of Jesus Christ, a select group of people were chosen by God and led by His law. They were the Jews, God's chosen people. The law was designed to lead them to the Messiah, the Christ.

> Therefore the law was our tutor to bring us to Christ, that we might be justified by faith. (Galatians 3:24)

The Jews were tutored by way of the tabernacle of Moses and through life in Canaan under the leadership of the priests and kings of Israel. Their law spoke of a Messiah to come, and their faith was placed in His future arrival. When Jesus came to earth, He acknowledged that He was the Messiah when He spoke to the woman at the well.

> The woman said to Him, "I know that Messiah is coming" (who is called Christ). "When He comes, He will tell us all things." Jesus said to her, "I who speak to you am He." (John 4:25, 26)

> Yet many of the Jews did not recognize Him as the Messiah.

> He was in the world, and the world was made through Him, and the world did not know Him. He came to His own, and His own did not receive Him. (John 1:10, 11)

> Those who accepted Him as the Messiah were given the right to become sons of God.

> But as many as received Him, to them He gave the right to become children of God, even to those who believe in His name: who were born, not of blood, nor of the will of the flesh, nor of the will of man, but of God. (John 1:12)

Christ's death on the cross gave everyone—both Jews and Gentiles—the opportunity to enter into the kingdom of heaven. The third day of creation was centered on preparing a group of people to enter the promised kingdom of heaven, grow in Christ, and bear fruit. These are the disciples who were destined to follow Jesus Christ.

The Dry Land

> Then God said, "Let the waters under the heavens be gathered together into one place, and let the dry land appear"; and it was so. (Genesis 1:9)

As previously mentioned, the waters under the heavens are the peoples, tribes, and nations of the earth. These groups of people are compared to "seas," for like seas, they are always in turmoil. And like the fish of the sea, the people move about with little or no direction. As chaos develops from this lack of direction, the seas become stormy and frightening. The dry land allowed for stability.

Stability was established by introducing the law. God chose a group of people out of the seas of the world and placed them on firm ground. He gave them laws to abide by and gave them direction through His prophets.

The concept of land versus sea is important in order to understand prophecy in Revelation 13, where the two beasts appear. The first rises from the sea, and the second rises from the land. The first beast shall rise from the sea of nations, and the second shall rise from within the Jews who are under the law.

Canaan

Egypt was like a sea. The Lord brought His people out of the sea and into a wilderness. It was here that God's people were introduced to His law. After wandering through the wilderness, the law brought them to Canaan—the promised land, a dry land.

Canaan did not typify Eden nor the Father's kingdom. Canaan was a type of the kingdom of heaven. It was a place where people had to struggle with good and evil, mainly with the spirit of disobedience. Disobedience was the reason mankind was removed from the Garden of Eden. Prosperity in Canaan depended on how well the people adhered to the law. Old Testament books such as Judges and 1 and 2 Kings clearly demonstrate this struggle with following God's law. When Israel worshipped idols, they were punished and required to make atonement for the sin, often through an animal sacrifice. When they destroyed the idols and set their hearts on God, they were rewarded. Israel went through many cycles of punishments and rewards.

... Who brought us up out of the land of Egypt, who led us through the wilderness, through a land of deserts and pits, through a land of drought and the shadow of death, through a land that no one crossed and where no one dwelt? I brought you into a bountiful country to eat its fruit and its goodness. But when you entered, you defiled My land and made My heritage an abomination. (Jeremiah 2:6, 7)

Section II – The Purpose of the Law

In order to maintain stability, the law served two purposes. First, God's law was designed to guide His people to Him.

But before faith came, we were kept under guard by the law, kept for the faith which would afterward be revealed. Therefore the law was our tutor to bring us to Christ, that we might be justified by faith. (Galatians 3:23, 24)

This created hope of a greater thing to come. The second purpose of the law was to establish the knowledge of sin.

For by the law is the knowledge of sin. (Romans 3:20)

The law set forth an orderly way of life until the time in which the hope of the Messiah's coming was to be fulfilled. The Ten Commandments built the foundational principles of the law. The first commandment states that there is only one true God:

I am the Lord your God, who brought you out of the land of Egypt, out of the house of bondage. You shall have no gods before Me. (Exodus 20:2, 3)

The second commandment states that the gods of the world are idols, and that it is prohibited to bow down to images of such gods.

You shall not make for yourself any carved image, or any likeness of anything that is in heaven above, or that is in the earth beneath, or that is in the water under the earth; you shall not bow down to them nor serve them... (Exodus 20:4, 5)

The third commandment states that we should not take the name of our God lightly. His name should not be used foolishly.

> You shall not take the name of the Lord your God in vain, for the Lord will not hold him guiltless who takes His name in vain. (Exodus 20:7)

The fourth commandment states the principle of God's rest.

> Remember the Sabbath day, to keep it holy. Six days you shall labor and do all your work, but the seventh day is the Sabbath of the Lord your God. In it you shall do no work... (Exodus 20:8–10)

The fifth commandment states that we are to respect and obey our parents.

> Honor your father and your mother, that your days may be long upon the land which the Lord your God is giving you. (Exodus 20:12)

The sixth commandment states that human life should be highly valued.

> You shall not murder. (Exodus 20:13)

The seventh commandment states that we are to live morally and honor marriage. This includes avoiding adultery, fornication, pornography, lust, and sexual uncleanness.

> You shall not commit adultery. (Exodus 20:14)

The eighth commandment states that we should not take things that belong to another.

> You shall not steal. (Ex. 20:15)

The ninth commandment states that we should not lie or bring false accusations against others.

You shall not bear false witness against your neighbor. (Exodus 20:16)

The tenth commandment states that we should not lust after or desire the things that belong to our neighbor.

You shall not covet your neighbor's house; you shall not covet your neighbor's wife, nor his manservant, nor his maidservant, nor his ox, nor his donkey, nor anything that is your neighbor's. (Exodus 20:17)

If abided, these laws allowed the people to live in harmony firmly planted on dry ground.

Section III – Foreordained

The third day of creation set the stage for the sixth day of creation. For on the sixth day...

... God said, "Let Us make man in Our image, according to Our likeness..." (Genesis 1:26)

With the arrival of the Messiah and the setting up of the kingdom of heaven, man had the opportunity to be conformed to the image of God. Humanity at last had access to perfection without the requirement of animal sacrifice.

To those who are called according to His purpose. For whom He foreknew, He also predestined to be conformed to the image of His Son... (Romans 8:28, 29)

Just as He chose us in Him before the foundation of the world, that we should be holy and without blame before Him in love, having predestined us to adoption as sons by Jesus Christ to Himself, according to the good pleasure of His will. (Ephesians 1:4, 5)

Beloved, now we are children of God; and it has not yet been revealed what we shall be, but we know that when He is revealed, we shall be like Him, for we shall see Him as He is. (John 3:2)

The people of Israel were prepared in advance for the appearance of the Messiah, and they were responsible for preserving the Old Testament doctrine until His arrival.

> This day the Lord your God commands you to observe these statutes and judgments; therefore you shall be careful to observe them with all your heart and with all your soul. Today you have proclaimed the Lord to be your God, and that you will walk in His ways and keep His statutes, His commandments, and His judgments, and that you will obey His voice. Also today the Lord has proclaimed you to be His special people, just as He has promised you, that you should keep all His commandments, and that He will set you high above all nations which He has made, in praise, in name, and in honor, and that you may be a holy people to the Lord your God, just as He has spoken. (Deuteronomy 26:16–19)

The doctrine of law and the prophets was based on the golden rule: do unto others as you would have them do unto you.

> Therefore, whatever you want men to do to you, do also to them, for this is the law and the prophets. (Matthew 7:12)

While some theologians feel that Christ's arrival abolished the law, this doctrine of righteous living was not destroyed when Jesus appeared.

> Do not think that I came to destroy the law and the prophets. I did not come to destroy but to fulfill. (Matthew 5:17)

Section IV – Righteousness

The Earth's Garment

> And the earth brought forth grass, the herb that yields seed according to its kind... (Genesis 1:12)

When flourishing, grass, herbs, and trees are green in appearance. When there is plenty of rain, the earth is green with vegetation. Green grass is like the earth's garment. It covers the land like a garment covers the body. In a time of drought, the earth is parched and brown, reflecting death. When God's people were in obedience to Him, the rain fell and the earth was green. When in disobedience, the rain was withheld, and the earth became a parched wilderness.

In 1 Kings, Ahab provoked the Lord to anger by fabricating an idol (16:33). As a result, Elijah proclaimed a drought would come as punishment (17:1). Following the destruction of the prophets of Baal on Mount Carmel (18:40), the rain returned (18:45) as affirmation of their return to obedience.

The Lord reinforces this principle of earthly blessing and curses from His comments in the book of Jeremiah.

> Thus says the Lord: "Cursed is the man who trusts in man and makes flesh his strength, whose heart departs from the Lord. For he shall be like a shrub in the desert, and shall not see when good comes, but shall inhabit the parched places in the wilderness, in a salt land which is not inhabited. Blessed is the man who trusts in the Lord, and whose hope is the Lord. For he shall be like a tree planted by the waters, which spreads out its roots by the river, and will not fear when heat comes; but its leaf will be **green**, and will not be anxious in the year of drought, nor will cease from yielding fruit." (Jeremiah 17:5–8)

These verses point out the relationship of a righteous person as being a green tree bearing much fruit. It is the heart that the Lord examines. It is by righteousness that the Lord shall judge.

But with righteousness He shall judge the poor... (Isaiah 11:4)

The condition of the heart is a measure of righteousness, for a heart that seeks holiness reflects the pure heart of God. And a wicked heart seeks selfish ways.

The heart is deceitful above all things, and desperately wicked; Who can know it? I, the Lord, search the heart, I test the mind, even to give every man according to his ways, and according to the fruit of his doings. (Jeremiah 17:9, 10)

When the Pharaoh of Egypt hardened his heart against God and would not let God's people go, the Lord struck the land with plagues and disasters of all sorts. The eighth plague involved locusts that devoured all the green vegetation.

Previously there had been no such locusts as they, nor shall there be such after them. For they covered the face of the whole earth, so that the land was darkened; and they ate every herb of the land and all the fruit of the trees which the hail had left. So there remained nothing green on the trees or on the plants of the field throughout all the land of Egypt. (Exodus 10:14, 15)

There appears to be a strong relationship between the color green and righteousness. This righteousness is seen around God's throne.

And there was a rainbow around the throne, in appearance like an emerald. (Revelation 4:3)

An emerald is green. Some theologians associate righteousness with the color white. However, white is associated with the word "salvation."

He who overcomes shall be clothed in white garments... (Revelation 3:5)

Those who overcome shall be saved and given white garments to wear. Fine linen also represents righteousness, for the fine linen in the garments speaks of the righteous acts of those who inherit salvation.

> And to her it was granted to be arrayed in fine linen, clean and bright, for the fine linen is the righteous acts of the saints. (Revelation 19:8)

When we look at the intricate pattern of creation, nature appears as a finely woven cloth, beautiful and breathtaking.

Eden

The Garden of Eden typified the condition of a person whose heart was in tune with the heart of God. It was a land covered with lush green vegetation representing a place of peace and righteousness and blessing.

> And out of the ground the Lord God made every tree grow that is pleasant to the sight and good for food... (Genesis 2:9)

In this garden God walked and talked with Adam and Eve.

> And they heard the sound of the Lord God walking in the garden in the cool of the day...Then the Lord God called to Adam and said to him, "Where are you?" (Genesis 3:8, 9)

When Adam disobeyed God, he was cast out of the garden and the ground was cursed

> ... Cursed is the ground for your sake... (Genesis 3:17)

Any offering made from this ground was not acceptable.

> And in the process of time it came to pass that Cain brought an offering of the fruit of the ground to the Lord... but He did not respect Cain and his offering... (Genesis 4:3, 5)

After being cast out of Eden, a type of the Father's kingdom, mankind operated according to his own righteousness and his offering was not acceptable to God. It was not until after the great flood that God removed the curse from the ground so that man could make peace with Him.

> ... I will never again curse the ground for man's sake... (Genesis 8:21)

This set the stage for instituting the law which the Lord established through Moses. The law set the mind of humanity on God through obedience. It was designed to bring people back to Eden by way of the kingdom of heaven—the body of Christ. The law would serve as a tutor to bring Israel to Christ.

Yielding Seed According to its Kind

Seeds are essential to growth. Genesis 1:12 references yielding seed of its kind:

> And the earth brought forth grass, the herb that yields seed according to its kind... (Genesis 1:12)

The law and hope of redemption through the Messiah along with a system of kings, priests, and prophets enabled God's chosen people to preserve their way of life from generation to generation. The law of righteousness remains the same today as it did when Moses handed down the Ten Commandments to the Israelites.

Preserving seed serves two purposes. First, it preserved the law and Israel until the time when the hope of redemption was fulfilled at the Messiah's coming. Second, it preserved Israel to this day. The law and the prophets were fulfilled by Jesus, and they remain in Christianity today. Righteousness and the fruit of the Spirit are still yielding seed according to its kind.

Fruit

> And the tree that yields fruit, whose seed is in itself according to its kind... (Genesis 1:12)

The tree of life represented the doctrine that set the heart towards God. This same tree bears the fruit of the Spirit.

> But the fruit of the Spirit is love, joy, peace, longsuffering, kindness, goodness, faithfulness, gentleness, self-control... (Galatians 5:22, 23)

Much like the natural fruit we eat, the seed within each fruit of the Spirit is the word of God. Different fruit portray different aspects of the word of God. Disciples who dwell in the kingdom of heaven are like trees bearing fruit of the Spirit—each with a different purpose.

Yet there is not just one tree mentioned in Scripture. Back in the Garden of Eden, the tree of the knowledge of good and evil represented doctrine. By eating of this fruit, mankind set his heart upon a mixture of the evil ways of the world and God's righteousness. Suddenly evil waged war against God's perfect creation. The nature of this tree was that of Satan—eager for power.

> No tree in the garden of God was like it in beauty...You were in Eden the garden of God... I made it beautiful with a multitude of branches, so that all the trees of Eden envied it, that were in the garden of God...Your heart was lifted up because of your beauty; you corrupted your wisdom for the sake of your splendor... For you have said in your heart: I will ascend into heaven, I will exalt my throne above the stars of God... I will ascend above the heights of the clouds, I will be like the Most High....its heart was lifted up in its height, therefore... I have driven it out for its wickedness. (Ezekiel 28:31; Isaiah 14)

God had instructed Adam and Eve not to eat of the tree of the knowledge of good and evil, for He knew the consequences of such an action.

> And the Lord God commanded the man, saying, "Of every tree of the garden you may eat; but of the tree of knowledge

of good and evil you shall not eat, for in the day that you eat of it you shall surely die." (Genesis 2:16, 17)

The Hebrew word for knowledge in this passage is *daath*. It means to have knowledge of something in a cunning or witting way. It is skillful use of knowledge. The serpent used this kind of skill to deceive Eve into eating of the tree of the knowledge of good and evil.

Now the serpent was more cunning than any beast of the field which the Lord God had made... (Genesis 3:1)

The serpent had knowledge of God's commandment not to eat of this particular tree. Yet he took this knowledge and added a little twist to it. He took good doctrine and perverted it with evil doctrine. The result was that Eve ended up deceived into eating of the doctrine of truth and error.

But I fear, lest somehow, as the serpent deceived Eve by his craftiness, so your minds may be corrupted from the simplicity that is in Christ. (2 Corinthians 11:3)

Notice how the serpent uses his cunning ways as he appeals to Eve's vanity:

... And he said to the woman, "Has God indeed said, 'You shall not eat of every tree of the garden?'" And the woman said to the serpent, "We may eat the fruit of the trees of the garden; but of the fruit of the tree which is in the midst of the garden, God said, 'You shall not eat it, lest you die.'" And the serpent said to the woman, "You will not surely die." (Genesis 3:1–4)

The serpent's initial questioning began with the woman's knowledge of God's word. In other words, Satan is saying, "Did God really say that?" Eve responds by quoting God's commandment to the serpent. The serpent then convinces Eve that God only commanded them not to eat of the tree because God is keeping something from her. Upon yielding to the serpent's deception, she finds pleasure in the doctrine of truth and error by eating the forbidden fruit.

In his shame, man received his consequence and was cast out of the garden. Even today Satan uses this same tactic in his attempt to draw people away from God. The story of Adam and Eve is typical of what happens to people when they compromise true doctrine with the ways of the world.

The True Vine

John spoke of bearing fruit in his narration about the vine and the branches.

> I am the vine, you are the branches. He who abides in Me, and I in him, bears much fruit; for without Me you can do nothing. (John 15:5)

Bearing fruit has two aspects to it. One aspect is acquiring the mind of Christ. The other is sharing the salvation message to others, for the seed, or word of God that is in you, will produce more disciples.

> If you abide in Me, and My words abide in you, you will ask what you desire, and it shall be done for you. By this My Father is glorified, that you bear much fruit; so you will be My disciples. (John 15:7, 8)

When Peter presented the word of salvation, three thousand souls were added to the Church, as recounted in the book of Acts.

> Then those who gladly received his word were baptized; and that day about three thousand souls were added to them. (Acts 2:41)

Certainly the message of salvation is a powerful one.

The Tabernacle of David

Christ took Canaan into a higher dimension when He established the kingdom of heaven. This spiritual dimension was based on man's heart attitude towards God, not just on obedience to the law. It was a higher plain of spiritual understanding of God's ways beyond that of the Levitical law. David demonstrated this added dimension by way of his tabernacle on Mount Zion. He introduced a new form of worship aside from the worship still being performed in Moses' tabernacle.

> So David and all the house of Israel brought up the ark of the Lord with shouting and with the sound of the trumpet... And as the ark of the Lord came into the City of David, Saul's daughter... saw King David leaping and whirling before the Lord... (2 Samuel 6:15, 16)

> Christ's righteousness was tied to David's form of worship.

> "Behold, the days are coming," says the Lord, "That I will raise to David a Branch of righteousness; a King shall reign and prosper, and execute judgment and righteousness in the earth." (Jeremiah 23:5)

Christ was the righteous branch. David's form of worship was the key to the kingdom of heaven. It became known as the key of David.

> And to the angel of the church in Philadelphia write, "These things says He who is holy, He who is true, He who has the key of David, He who opens and no one shuts, and shuts and no one opens." (Revelation 3:7)

The key of David was the right heart attitude toward God. God's people who followed the law gave the outward appearance of living according to the attributes of God, but God was not just interested in the outward appearance of a person. He is also interested in the heart. Matters of the heart are God's primary concern. The condition of Canaan represented the overall condition of the heart of God's people. Genesis opens up with this concern. The earth was void of the knowledge of God and darkness was upon the face of the deep, that is, the heart of man. This was where Christ's sacrifice came to take the punishment of the darkened hearts.

Section V – At Day's End

Sin is the willful or deliberate act of breaking God's law. Iniquity is the weakness that is inherent in us, a sin nature that breeds the transgression. Prior to Christ, man's conscience becomes alerted to the ways of darkness by way of the law. The law served as a tutor to bring man to Christ.

Upon entering the body of Christ, the disciples become alerted to the ways of darkness through the heart of David, and prosperity will be seen in the land where they dwell. The rain will fall when it is needed, and like fruit trees, they will bear fruit. They shall exhibit love, joy, peace, longsuffering, kindness, goodness, faithfulness, gentleness, and self-control. They will be the envy of their neighbors. The seas shall suffer storms, but the righteous shall dwell in safety.

Thus ends the third day concerning that which is good and that which is evil as established through the first sin of mankind—a sin that separated us from God. But God had plans of reconciliation as he provided entrance into His kingdom.

So the evening and the morning were the third day. (Genesis 1:13)

Chapter 4

The Fourth Day

Section I – Feed My Sheep

During the first day of creation, God introduced knowledge and understanding of His way of living. This was followed by the second day of creation which established a place of learning, the kingdom of heaven. The third day of creation addressed students who were given the opportunity to enter the school. A school requires an authoritative structure to rule over the students. This structure is established under the fourth day of creation.

Administrators and instructors are needed to teach knowledge and understanding of the ways of God.

> And I will give you shepherds according to My heart, who will feed you with knowledge and understanding. (Jeremiah 3:15)

> So when they had eaten breakfast, Jesus said to Simon Peter, "Simon, son of Jonah, do you love Me more than these?" He said to Him, "Yes Lord; You know that I love You." He said to Him, "Feed My lambs." He said to him again a second

time, "Simon, son of Jonah, do you love Me?" He said to Him, "Yes Lord; You know that I love You." He said to him, "Tend My sheep." He said to him the third time, "Simon, son of Jonah, do you love Me?" Peter was grieved because He said to him the third time, "Do you love Me?" And he said to Him, "Lord, You know all things; You know that I love You." Jesus said to him, "Feed My sheep." (John 21:15–17)

This teaching ministry—feeding the sheep—consists of those mentioned in Ephesians 4.

And He Himself gave some to be apostles, some prophets, some evangelist, and some pastors and teachers, for the equipping of the saints for the work of ministry, for the edifying of the body of Christ, till we all come to the unity of the faith and the knowledge of the Son of God, to a perfect man, to the measure of the stature of Christ; that we should no longer be children, tossed to and fro and carried about with every wind of doctrine, by the trickery of men, in the cunning craftiness by which they lie in wait to deceive, but, speaking the truth in love, may grow up in all things into Him who is the head—Christ. (Ephesians 4:12–15)

The original twelve apostles were given the responsibility to preserve the true doctrine of Christ in their teaching.

And He said, "To you it has been given to know the mysteries of the kingdom of God, but to the rest it is given in parables…" (Luke 8:10)

In the miracle involving the feeding of the five thousand, Jesus took two fish and five loaves, broke them, and instructed the twelve disciples to distribute the pieces to the multitudes. Twelve baskets of fragments were left over.

The significance of the numbers in this event holds some key truths. The two fish stood for knowledge and understanding of the ways of God that were being fed to the multitudes by Jesus' disciples. The five loaves represented the five ingredients that make up the kingdom of heaven, which stood for the doctrine of Jesus Christ. These ingredients were entrusted to the disciples. The disciples in turn fed the mysteries of the kingdom of heaven to the multitudes. The twelve baskets left over stood for each of the twelve apostles who, after feeding the multitudes, still retain knowledge, understanding, and mysteries of the kingdom and are able to feed others.

Jesus comments on this miracle when He cautions His disciples on the doctrine of the Pharisees and Sadducees.

> "Do you not yet understand, or remember the five loaves of the five thousand and how many baskets you took up?... How is it you do not understand that I did not speak to you concerning bread?—But you should beware of the leaven of the Pharisees and Sadducees." Then they understood that He did not tell them to beware of the leaven of bread, but of the doctrine of the Pharisees and Sadducees. (Matthew 16:9, 11, 12)

The five loaves in the feeding of the five thousand symbolized the doctrine of Jesus Christ in relationship to the kingdom of heaven. In reference to the church at Ephesus in Revelation, this true doctrine was used to test those who proclaimed to be apostles.

> ... And you have tested those who say they are apostles and are not, and found them liars. (Revelation 2:2)

As Christians, we are ruled by the Bible and the authority behind it.

> All scripture is given by inspiration of God, and is profitable for doctrine, for reproof, for correction, for instruction in righteousness, that the man of God may be complete, thoroughly equipped for every good work. (2 Timothy 3:16, 17)

Thus enters the fourth day—the authority that governs the Church, the kingdom of heaven, the body of Christ, the school.

> Then God said, "Let there be lights in the firmament of the heavens to divide the day from the night; and let them be

for signs and seasons, and for days and years; and let them be for lights in the firmament of the heavens to give light on the earth"; and it was so. Then God made two great lights: the greater light to rule the day, and the lesser light to rule the night. He made the stars also. God set them in the firmament of the heavens to give light on the earth, and to rule over the day and over the night, and to divide the light from the darkness. And God saw that it was good. (Genesis 1:14–18)

Section II – Lights

The above passage of Scripture implies that the lights are the sun, moon, and stars, the greater light being the sun and the lesser light being the moon. Lights are helpers or teachers that serve to guide disciples as they dwell in the kingdom of heaven. Such teachers are needed to help disciples discern between that which is good and that which is evil. Symbology would imply that the sun represents the Father, the moon represents the Son, and the stars represent angels who are ministering spirits, or perhaps Christian leaders carrying the light of the gospel of Jesus Christ to the world.

These symbols are used to describe the woman in Revelation 12.

> Now a great sign appeared in heaven: a woman clothed with the sun, with the moon under her feet, and on her head a garland of twelve stars. (Revelation 12:1)

The woman could very well represent the bride of Christ who is clothed with the glory of the Father and is standing on the testimony of Jesus Christ. The stars represent the light of the doctrine of Jesus Christ as preserved by the twelve apostles. The woman is governed by and walks in this doctrine.

The Greater Light

The sun, being the greater light, represents the Father.

For the Lord God is a sun and shield... (Psalms 84:11)

This is the message which we have heard from Him and declare to you, that God is light and in Him is no darkness at all. (1 John 1:5)

This light contains truth concerning the righteous ways of God. As the earth turns, man is exposed to truth (day) and error (night). This is truth. This is error. This is truth. This is error. This goes on and on, 365 times a year for as many years as one lives. Where man is clearly shown the difference between truth and error, he has no excuse when he chooses error.

For since the creation of the world His invisible attributes are clearly seen, being understood by the things that are made, even His eternal power and Godhead, so that they are without excuse. (Romans 1:20)

Following the crucifixion of Christ, we were not just left with the inspired written word of God. Jesus promised to ask the Father to provide another guide to help us in our growth. This guide was the light of the Spirit of God the Father.

And I will ask the Father, and He will give you another Helper, that He may be with you forever; that is the Spirit of truth... But the Helper, the Holy Spirit, whom the Father will send in My name, He will teach you all things. (John 14:16, 17, 26)

Prior to His ascension, Jesus told His disciples to tarry in Jerusalem where they were to personally receive the power of the Holy Spirit.

... He commanded them not to depart from Jerusalem, but wait for the Promise of the Father... But you shall receive power when the Holy Spirit has come upon you... (Acts 1:4, 8)

The *rhema*—the spoken understanding of the Spirit—began to flow to them when they had gathered in Jerusalem.

And suddenly there came a sound from heaven, as of a rushing wind, and it filled the whole house where they were sitting. Then there appeared to them divided tongues of fire, and one sat upon each of them. And they were all filled with the Holy Spirit and began to speak with other tongues, as the Spirit gave them utterance. (Acts 2:2–4)

The baptism of the Holy Spirit was not restricted to only those in the upper room.

Then those who gladly received his word were baptized; and that day about three thousand souls were added to them. (Acts 2:41)

The Lesser Light

The moon, being the lesser light, represents the Son.

It shall be established forever like the moon, even like the faithful witness in the sky. (Psalms 89:37)

This passage describes Jesus as the faithful witness to the power and glory of the Father.

And from Jesus Christ, the faithful witness... (Revelation 1:5)

As a witness to God's power, Jesus considered the Father to be greater than Him.

I am going to the Father, for My Father is greater than I. (John 14:28)

In examining these passages, the Father is the greater light. Jesus is the lesser light. The moon does not generate light of its own. It reflects light from the sun. The Son is a reflection of the Father.

Jesus said to Him... He who has seen Me has seen the Father. (John 14:9)

Jesus emphasized that the things He taught came from the Father.

> And that I do nothing of Myself; but as My Father taught Me, I speak these things. (John 8:28)

> For I have not spoken on My own authority; but the Father who sent Me gave Me a command, what I should say and what I should speak... just as the Father has told Me, so I speak. (John 12:49, 50)

When He was addressed as the "good teacher" by a particular ruler, He chastised the ruler for not recognizing that His teachings came from the Father.

> Now a certain ruler asked Him, saying, 'Good Teacher, what shall I do to inherit eternal life?' So Jesus said to him, 'Why do you call me good? No one is good but One, that is, God.' (Luke 18:18, 19)

The ruler did not perceive Jesus as speaking on behalf of the Father nor as being the Son of God. The ruler perceived Him merely as a wise teacher of Israel. Had the ruler understood Jesus to be the Son of God, Jesus would not have chastised him for calling Him good. In Genesis 1, light was considered to be good.

> And God saw the light, that it was good; and God divided the light from the darkness. (Genesis 1:4)

Since Jesus is the light of the world, it stands to reason that He would also be considered good.

> In Him is life, and the life was the light of men. (John 1:4)

> Then Jesus spoke to them again, saying, "I am the light of the world. He who follows Me shall not walk in darkness, but have the light of life." (John 8:12)

In order to perceive Him as good, one must see Him as God and as the light of the world. Jesus represented the true characteristics of the Father, for He was one with the Father, yet also with a purpose different from that of the Father.

Jesus is God

One of the most difficult relationships to describe in the Bible is that of the Father and Son. They are spoken of separately, yet they are said to be one and the same. They are said to have different personalities, yet they are one. How can this contradiction be?

One way to explain the relationship of the Son to the Father is to use mathematical terms of sets and subsets. A set contains two or more elements. A portion of these elements is a subset. The entirety of God is a set of all His attributes. A subset of these attributes is the Word (*logos*) of God. The elements or attributes of the subset are also found in the set.

The personality of the Father is based on His entirety, or the single set. The personality of the Son is based on the subset of the Father. This makes the personality of the Father and Son different. If God is perfect, the elements of the subset, being the Son, are also perfect. Therefore, the nature of the Son is perfect, being a subset of perfection.

When we pursue perfection in the kingdom of heaven, the perfection is a subset of the body of Christ. Since each person views God differently, each person perceives a different subset of divine elements. Some of these subsets may overlap each other. Nevertheless, the perfected subset, being common to some of the attributes of God's perfect nature, becomes a son. Therefore, when we are in the kingdom of heaven, the perfect nature in us qualifies us as sons of God.

> But when the fullness of the time had come, God sent forth His Son...to redeem those who were under the law, that we might receive the adoption as sons. And because you are sons, God has sent forth the Spirit of His Son into your

hearts... and if a son, then an heir of God through Christ. (Galatians 4:4–7)

This is not to say that the complete set of elements in man's character is perfect. Only a subset is perfect. It is this perfect subset that qualifies us to be called sons of God. As the imperfections disappear, man's overall nature approaches perfection in terms of God's nature as revealed through His Son, the Lord Jesus Christ.

If man, being imperfect, was to attempt to attach a name to God in order to describe His perfect nature, he would fail. When Moses inquired as to the name of God, God responded by saying, "I AM WHO I AM" in Exodus 3:14.

When theologians claim that Jesus is God and at the same time state that Jesus is not God, there is an element of intellectual correctness to this. The Word, as we know it, is God, but not the entire nature of God. The Father is the totality of God. The Son is the expression or Word of God that we know.

Man, being imperfect, cannot fully comprehend God. God is to a person to the degree by which He is revealed to that person. God is what you know about Him. What a person thinks he knows about God may not necessarily be correct. When asked to describe God, each person will often respond with a different perception. Each person's concept of God is different, just as no two snowflakes are alike.

For example, place a covered box with different colored sides on a table. Sit two people on opposite sides of the box. Remove the cover and question each person as to what color the box is. Each one will respond with a different answer. If the box is viewed from a different position, a new perspective of the box is revealed. The same holds true for God. If we view God from different aspects, our perception of Him changes. The more aspects we are able to see, the greater our knowledge is of Him.

Regardless of how the box is perceived, the box is still a multicolored box. So, too, God doesn't change because we perceive Him differently. He remains the same. His attributes do not change.

"For I am the Lord, I do not change." (Malachi 3:6)

Using this same illustration, if the box is moved far away, we cannot see its characteristics clearly. The further we move from God, the less we know of Him. The closer we come to Him, the more we know Him.

Angels

The stars represent angels or Christian ministers carrying the light of the gospel. The relationship of angels to stars is mentioned in Revelation 1:20:

> The seven stars are the seven angels of the seven churches.

When looking at the composition of stars, they are flames of fire. In Hebrews 1:7, angels are represented as flames of fires.

> And of the angels He says: "Who makes His angels spirits and His ministers a flame of fire." (Hebrew 1:7)

Scripture tells us that angels are commissioned to serve as ministering spirits.

> Are they (angels) not all ministering spirits sent forth to minister for those who will inherit salvation? (Hebrew 1:14)

Unlike the moon that reflects light from the sun, light from a star emanates from itself. With this independence, an angel's word may not agree with the Father's word. Angels can teach false doctrine, much like Satan—the angel named Lucifer—did.

> But even if we, or an angel from heaven, preach any other gospel to you than what we have preached to you, let him be accursed. (Galatians 1:8)

Therefore, it is necessary to test spirits who communicate in whatever fashion.

> Beloved, do not believe every spirit, but test the spirits... (1 John 4:1)

Similar to that of the angels, Christians ministering the gospel of Jesus Christ are independent and may not be speaking the truth. They are to be tested as well to ensure the message aligns with Scripture.

Section III – Authority

With respect to authority, the Father is above the Son, the Son is above man, and the man is above the woman.

> But I want you to know that the head of every man is Christ, the head of woman is man, and the head of Christ is God. (1 Corinthians 11:3)

Together, the husband and wife rule over their children.

> Children, obey your parents in all things, for this is well pleasing to the Lord. (Colossians 3:20)

> Honor your father and mother... that it may be well with you and you may live long on the earth. (Ephesians 6:2, 3)

Because they are created beings, angels are also subject to the authority of Christ.

> Who has gone into heaven and is at the right hand of God, angels and authorities and powers having been made subject to Him. (1 Peter 3:22)

Christ is the head of His body, the Church.

> For the husband is head of the wife, as also Christ is head of the church; and He is the Savior of the body. (Ephesians 5:23)

Church leaders are subject to Christ and are placed over the brethren to guide them in the ways of Christ.

> And we urge you, brethren, to recognize those who labor among you, and are over you in the Lord and admonish you,

and to esteem them very highly in love for their work's sake. Be at peace among yourselves. (1 Thessalonians 5:12, 13)

Ministering spirits, by nature being instructors or guides, rank above the disciples as well as other men.

What is man that you are mindful of him...You made him a little lower than the angels... (Hebrews 2:7)

As such, the disciple should respect the authority of angels. However, a disciple should always test the spirit and make sure that the angel's word does not contradict the holy Scriptures. False doctrine does not have authority over man.

The hierarchy of headship gives mankind guidance in how to live. In the area of government, Christ reigns over the leaders of nations who are in turn over local governments who are in turn over the citizens. As disciples, we must obey the laws of the land and submit ourselves to every ordinance. 1 Peter 2 and Romans 13 cover this area of politics in detail.

Therefore submit yourselves to every ordinance of man for the Lord's sake, whether to the king as supreme, or to governors, as to those who are sent by him for the punishment of evildoers and for the praise of those who do good. (1 Peter 2:13, 14)

Let every soul be subject to the governing authorities. For there is no authority except from God, and the authorities that exist are appointed by God. Therefore whoever resists the authority resists the ordinance of God, and those who resist will bring judgment on themselves. (Romans 13:1, 2)

When it comes to business relationships, we are to serve our employers well and yield to their authority.

Servants, obey in all things your masters according to the flesh... in sincerity of heart... for you serve the Lord Christ. (Colossians 3:22–24)

Rebellion against authority causes ministry to suffer. Ministers who rebel against God's principals are subject to removal from their positions. In response to Saul's rebellion, the kingdom was taken from Saul and handed to David.

> But now your kingdom shall not continue. The Lord has sought for Himself a man after His own heart, and the Lord has commanded him to be commander over His people, because you have not kept what the Lord commanded you. (1 Samuel 13:14)

Section IV – Suppression of Truth

The early church, as demonstrated in the book of Acts, testified to the Lord's great power. The word was confirmed with signs that followed. Demons were driven out and healings were recounted. However, subtle and gradual changes took place in the church as a result of a mixture of Christianity with pagan religions and worldly influences. The apostolic and prophetic ministry seemed to slowly disappear, along with baptism in the Holy Spirit and spiritual gifts. Local church autonomy gave way to larger churches, and eventually, Christianity became the religion of the state and dominated by the Roman Church.

Under the leadership of the Roman Church, the light of truth was severely compromised. Rome became the final authority in church matters. Truth was hidden under a basket, and people lived in what became known as the Dark Ages—a period of stagnation and decline.

However, God began restoring divine principles and truths through a remnant of people who apposed the Roman Church. One of the most notable individuals was Martin Luther, who reinstated biblically-supported "justification by faith." This was followed by the Anabaptists who instituted baptism by full emersion. John Wesley pushed holiness. This was followed by divine healings and the outpouring of the Holy Spirit in various revivals.

Section V – Baptized in the Holy Spirit

And it shall come to pass afterward that I will pour out My Spirit on all flesh; your sons and your daughters shall prophesy, your old men shall dream dreams, your young men shall see visions; and also on My menservants and on My maidservants I will pour out My Spirit in those days. (Joel 2:28, 29)

The gift of the Holy Spirit was promised to those who decided to follow Jesus.

Then Peter said to them, "Repent, and let every one of you be baptized in the name of Jesus Christ for the remission of sins; and you shall receive the gift of the Holy Spirit. For the promise is to you and to your children, and to all who are afar off, as many as the Lord our God will call." (Acts 2:38, 39)

The Spirit of God makes the words of the Bible real and personal to the Spirit-filled believer. Our Father wants us to understand the knowledge we have received.

But God has revealed them to us through His Spirit. For the Spirit searches all things, yes, the deep things of God. For what man knows the things of a man except the spirit of the man which is in him? Even so no one knows the things of God except the Spirit of God. Now we have received, not the spirit of the world, but the Spirit who is from God, that we might know the things that have been freely given to us by God. (1 Corinthians 2:10–12)

Section VI – The Commission

Being a "good student" is not enough. We must go beyond the first and greatest commandment of loving the Lord our God with all our heart and soul. We must fulfill the second commandment of loving our neighbor as ourselves by obeying the great commission, which is to embark on sharing the good news of Christ as Savior.

> Go therefore and make disciples of all the nations, baptizing them in the name of the Father and of the Son and of the Holy Spirit, teaching them to observe all things that I have commanded you... (Matthew 28:19, 20)

To assist in this endeavor, God provided instructors.

> And He Himself gave some to be apostles, some prophets, some evangelists, and some pastors and teachers, for the equipping of the saints for the work of ministry, for the edifying of the body of Christ, till we all come to the unity of the faith and the knowledge of the Son of God, to a perfect man, to the measure of the stature of the fullness of Christ; that we should no longer be children, tossed to and fro and carried about with every wind of doctrine, by the trickery of men... (Ephesians 4:11–14)

These various ministries are defined as follows:

Apostle:	One sent as a messenger or agent, the bearer of a commission, messenger
Prophet:	A spokesman for another, interpreter for a deity, a person gifted for the exposition of divine truth
Evangelist:	One who announces glad tidings, preacher of the gospel, teacher of the Christian religion
Pastor:	One who tends flocks or herds, a shepherd, herdsman, superintendent, guardian
Teacher:	Master, one who teaches, rabbi

The ministers of the gospel were small in number, yet the field ripe for the message numbered as the sand of the seashore. Therefore, Jesus trained ministers who would eventually grow as mustard seeds, both in stature and numbers. These ministers were to proclaim the news of the kingdom of heaven throughout all the earth. This process began with the "seventy" mentioned in Luke's gospel:

After these things the Lord appointed seventy others also, and sent them two by two before His face into every city and place where He Himself was about to go. Then He said to them, "The harvest truly is great, but the laborers are few"; therefore pray the Lord of the harvest to send out laborers into His harvest. (Luke 10:1, 2)

For this same purpose of calling forth laborers to spread the message of salvation, Jesus sent out His twelve disciples.

Then He said to His disciples, "The harvest truly is plentiful, but the laborers are few. Therefore pray the Lord of the harvest to send out laborers into His harvest." These twelve Jesus sent out and commanded them, saying... "and as you go, preach, saying, 'The kingdom of heaven is at hand.'" (Matthew 9:37, 38; 10:5, 7)

Not all ministries are the same. God provides various gifts to fulfill the function of ministry. The sum of all the various ministries will accomplish the complete will of God.

For as we have many members in one body, but all the members do not have the same function, so we, being many, are one body in Christ, and individually members of one another. Having then gifts differing according to the grace that is given to us, let us use them... (Romans 12:4–6)

In order to fulfill the commandment to love our neighbors as ourselves, each of us has a ministry to perform and a responsibility to carry out this ministry calling in a proper fashion.

For the equipping of the saints for the work of ministry, for the edifying of the body of Christ, till we all come to the unity of faith and the knowledge of the Son of God, to a perfect man, to the measure of the stature of the fullness of Christ.... that Christ may dwell in your hearts through faith; that you, being rooted and grounded in love, may be able to comprehend with all the saints what is the width and length and depth and height... to know the love of Christ which passes knowledge; that you may be filled with all the fullness of God. (Ephesians 3:12, 13, 17–19)

The five ministries called out in Ephesians 4 are sometimes referred to as the fivefold ministry. However, one must be careful not to infer that there are only five kinds of ministers, for the number "five" is generally associated with ministry—not limiting the number of ministries available. As will be pointed out later, the first five days of creation are five elements designed to prepare the disciples for ministry.

Section VII – Qualification of a Minister

In order to become an apostle, prophet, teacher, evangelist, or pastor, one must take advantage of the first five elements of creation. This requires attending a Christian school—a school that coexists within the body of Christ, the kingdom of heaven. This means that the disciple must accept the light, separate it from the darkness in his or her life, and grow as a holy, righteous individual. The qualification of a minister is described further in Ephesians 4.

> If indeed you have heard Him and have been taught by Him, as the truth is in Jesus: that you put off, concerning your former conduct, the old man which grows corrupt according to the deceitful lusts, and be renewed in the spirit of your mind, and that you put on the new man which was created according to God, in righteousness and true holiness. (Ephesians 4:21–24)

Those who minister should be mature disciples, shepherds raised up in the church to teach sound doctrine. Titus provides a good summary and doctrine on the qualifications of being a minister of God's word.

> A husband of one wife, having faithful children not accused of dissipation or insubordination... blameless, not self willed, not quick-tempered, not given to wine, not violent, not greedy for money, but hospitable, a lover of what is good,

sober-minded, just, holy, self-controlled, holding fast the faithful word as he has been taught, that he may be able, by sound doctrine, both to exhort and convict those who contradict. (Titus 1:6–9)

Section VIII – The Law of the Servants

One must put *logos* and *rhema* at work in the kingdom of heaven. *Logos* ministers knowledge. *Rhema* ministers understanding. With these two swords, one can minister with great wisdom. A person cannot minister in the image of God unless both *logos* and *rhema* are at work in his or her life. There must be a proper balance between these two swords in order to carry out an effective ministry.

Those who remain under the law do not operate with *rhema*—the Spirit. The Spirit offers relationship with God not based on law but based on grace. The only way to become free from the law is to operate with *rhema*. We are given a choice to operate under the law or to be free from the law.

In Exodus 21:6, concerning the law of the servants, if one purchased a Hebrew servant, the servant was to serve six years and in the seventh year he was to go free and pay nothing. If the servant loved his master and said, "I will not go out free," the master was to bring him to the judges and pierce his ear with an awl. Then the servant would serve his master forever.

Those who are under the bondage of the world and those who are under the bondage of the law are given the option to be free through Christ. The cost is covered by the price that Jesus paid on the cross. People are redeemed from the law and from sin by the blood of Jesus. So those who choose to remain a bond servant have no excuse; they are taken before the judges as witnesses.

1 John 5:6 points out that there are three who bear witness in heaven: the Father, the Word, and the Holy Spirit, and these three are one. Verse 8 says, "And there are three that bear witness on earth; the Spirit, the water, and the blood, and these three agree as one." These witnesses are the judges to whom the servant is taken when that person decides to remain with his or her master instead of going free.

In the letters to the churches in Revelation 2 and 3, the emphasis is on the word "overcome." The passage leading up to 1 John 5:6 also uses the word overcome:

> For whoever is born of God overcomes the world and who is the one who overcomes the world, but he who believes that Jesus is the Son of God? (1 John 5:4, 5)

Those who accept Christ have been set free from their former master. If a person decides to remain with his former master, he is given a mark and shall remain with that master according to Exodus 21:6.

We cannot serve two masters, for we will love one and hate the other. Christ is one master. The Antichrist is the other master. Whom shall you serve?

Section IX – God's Blessings

For those who so choose to enter into God's will, God is good to pour out His blessings on them. The blessings come in the form of protection, instruction, comfort, provision, and restoration. Ministers welcome this refreshing rain when they walk in the desolate valleys in the shadow of death.

> Yea, though I walk through the valley of the shadow of death, I will fear no evil; for you are with me (*protection*)... The Lord is my shepherd...He leads me in the path of righteousness (*instruction*) ... I shall not want... you prepare a table before me (*provision*)... He restores my soul (*restoration*)... Surely goodness and mercy shall follow me... You anoint my head with oil... Your rod and Your staff, they comfort me (*comfort*). (Psalms 23; italicized text added)

God's objective for mankind is complicated by the fact that His disciples have to physically survive in a world outside of the kingdom of heaven. It is a metaphysical existence. Spiritually, we are grafted into the vine and are encouraged to bear fruit. Physically, we live on the earth. This requires the need of food, shelter, clothing, and interacting with diverse peoples and social structures. Given all this, God is good to provide for His people—a people that He wishes to be made in His image.

Section X – At Day's End

As Christians, we dwell in the body of Christ. As such, it is imperative that during this time we are baptized in the Holy Spirit and that we seek to possess gifts of the Spirit to serve our Lord. When Jesus was crucified, the veil in the temple was rent from top to bottom. This gave us access to the Holy of Holies. There we can listen to the voice of God between the wings of the cherubim.

We have the Bible as our reference, and we have the Spirit of God available to guide and teach us at any moment. Although we have pastors, evangelists, and others who serve as our shepherds, the ultimate authority over the school, or kingdom of heaven, is God the Father, the Son, and the Holy Spirit. As our King, Jesus rules over the kingdom of heaven. We live under His rules and the authority behind them. This rule, authority, and power remains in the kingdom of heaven until Jesus hands the kingdom over to the Father.

> For He must reign till He has put all enemies under His feet. Then comes the end, when He delivers the kingdom to God the Father, when He puts an end to all rule and all authority and power. (1 Corinthians 15:24, 25)

The Dark Ages of ignorance are behind us. Our life is in Jesus, and He is the light of men. Walk with God daily. We, being a member of the body of Christ, are a light unto the world. As the Latin phrase goes, *"Nec temere nec timide."* Neither walk rashly nor timidly. Walk like a person with the mind of Christ.

So the evening and the morning were the fourth day. (Genesis 1:19)

Chapter 5

The Fifth Day

Section I – Tests

So, now we have a school filled with students who have access to knowledge and understanding of God's ways and an authoritative structure to guide and rule over them. However, a school would be remiss without one additional feature: tests.

> The heart is deceitful above all things, and desperately wicked; Who can know it? I, the Lord, search the heart, I **test** the mind, even to give every man according to his ways, and according to the fruit of his doings. (Jeremiah 17:9, 10; bolded for emphasis)

Body, Soul, and Spirit

Our human nature is threefold: body, soul, and spirit.

Now may the God of peace Himself sanctify you completely; and may your whole spirit, soul, and body be preserved blameless at the coming of our Lord Jesus Christ. (1 Thessalonians 5:23)

The body is the natural man that experiences physical senses such as that of seeing, hearing, tasting, smelling, and touching. The soul gives us identity. It contains our emotions, mind, and will; our inner feelings, intellect, and desires. The spirit is our invisible makeup that does not consist of matter. It is like the wind. The Greek word for spirit is *pneuma*, which means "wind." The soul of a person is contained in two entities: the flesh and the spirit. When a person dies, the natural body is separated from the spiritual body. While the natural body decays, the spirit lives on.

Remember now your Creator in the days of your youth... Then the dust will return to the earth as it was, and the spirit will return to God who gave it. (Ecclesiastes 12:1, 7)

An example of the spirit departing the body is shown in Luke 8 where Jesus restored life to the daughter of the ruler.

Then her spirit returned, and she arose immediately... (Luke 8:55)

The soul remains with the spiritual body. It is easily susceptible to change. The influences of the world will work upon the soul, creating the opportunity for one to sin. Upon deciding to follow Jesus, a person should reject worldly influences that may lead to sin and embrace a renewed spirit, the spirit of Christ.

Knowing this, that our old man was crucified with Him, that the body of sin might be done away with, that we should no longer be slaves of sin. (Romans 6:6)

Along with accepting Christ's identity, the Bible speaks of crucifying the flesh. Christians are to deny the flesh.

And those who are Christ's have crucified the flesh with its passions and desires. (Galatians 5:24)

Not only are worldly influences deadly, but the influences of the spiritual realm will also work upon the soul—whether for good or bad.

> Put on the whole armor of God, that you may be able to stand against the wiles of the devil. For we do not wrestle against flesh and blood, but against principalities, against powers, against rulers of the darkness of this age, against spiritual hosts of wickedness in the heavenly places. (Ephesians 6:11–12)

Scripture teaches that the Spirit and the flesh have a tendency to contend with each other.

> For the flesh lusts against the Spirit, and the Spirit against the flesh; and these are contrary to one another... (Galatians 5:17)

We are given a free choice to choose to be led by good or evil. The influences of the physical world and the spiritual realm become quite obvious as we attempt to fulfill that which we know to be right. Two battles must be fought to overcome sin—a spiritual battle and a fleshly battle. The good things of the world and of the spiritual realm attempt to push us towards righteousness. The converse holds as well; the evil things of the earthly and spiritual realms push us towards unrighteousness. The evil nature within these two forces seeks to draw our attention to wrong impulses. On the other hand, the good nature within these forces seeks to draw our attention to correct impulses. The Helper, the Holy Spirit of truth, exhorts us to draw our attention to the correct impulses.

> For I know that in me (that is, in my flesh) nothing good dwells... There is therefore now no condemnation to those who are in Christ Jesus, who do not walk according to the flesh, but according to the Spirit... For those who live according to the flesh set their minds on the things of the flesh, but those who live according to the Spirit, the things of the Spirit. For to be carnally minded is death, but to be

spiritually minded is life and peace... For as many as are led by the Spirit of God, these are sons of God. (Romans 7:18; 8:5, 6, 14)

Tests

Tests are tools that are used to check a student's progress and promote application of the lessons learned. For example, an algebra test will not only test for knowledge of particular skills, but it will test the ability to utilize the skills in a practical situation. Each test provides another experience from which the student can draw on to solve future problems. When a boxer attends a training camp, he is taught boxing skills and allowed to test his skills in sparring matches. Both the learned skills and the sparring matches serve to make him a better boxer.

In the kingdom of heaven, tests focus on the heart and its outward activity. The Holy Spirit will examine the light emitting from the face of the deep, and it will hover over the face of the waters and examine the outward workings.

When sinful ways draw us away from the path of righteousness, the lamp of the heart dims. In order to test the condition of the heart, God sets up test situations. He allows situations to occur by which we may choose between good and evil. These situations are facilitated by the presence of good and evil spirits in the spiritual realm, along with good and evil people of the world.

Thus enters the fifth day in which God created a background that enabled Him to test His disciples.

> Then God said, "Let the waters abound with an abundance of living creatures, and let birds fly above the earth across the face of the firmament of the heavens." So God created great sea creatures and every living thing that moves, with which the waters abounded, according to their kind. And God saw that it was good. And God blessed them, saying, "Be fruitful and multiply on the earth." (Genesis 1:20–22)

The Sea

The sea is an important illustrative tool that typifies the world.

> And he said to me, "The waters which you saw, where the harlot sits, are peoples, multitudes, nations, and tongues." (Revelation 17:15)

Fish

Fish are creatures that move about in the seas without direction.

> ...fish of the sea, like creeping things that have no ruler over them? (Habakkuk 1:14)

The fish are symbolic of those who reject God's law. The people who flounder around in the sea are those who roam the earth without direction. These are the ones Jesus wants to catch hold of.

> Now Jesus, walking by the Sea of Galilee, saw two brothers, Simon called Peter, and Andrew his brother, casting a net into the sea; for they were fishermen. And He said to them, "Follow Me, and I will make you fishers of men." (Matthew 4:18, 19)

Jesus often referred to unbelievers as fish, for He elected his disciples to be "fishers of men." Here Jesus shows a desire to reach out to unbelievers, for it is the will of God that all people be saved. We are to draw those who live in the sea to Christ. We are to rule over the men of the sea and influence them instead of them ruling over us and influencing us.

> Then God said, "... let them have dominion over the fish of the sea..." (Genesis 1:26)

Birds

Birds are symbolic of spirits. The Old Testament makes distinctions between clean and unclean birds.

All clean birds you may eat. But these you shall not eat: the eagle, the vulture, the buzzard... (Deuteronomy 14:11, 12)

Similarly, there are clean and unclean spirits. In the parable of the sower, birds represented the wicked one.

And the birds came and devoured them... then the wicked one comes and snatches away what was sown in his heart. (Matthew 13:4, 19)

The relationship of unclean spirits to unclean birds is also mentioned in Revelation.

And he cried mightily with a loud voice, saying, "Babylon the great is fallen, is fallen, and has become a habitation of demons, a prison for every foul spirit, and a cage for every unclean and hated bird!" (Revelation 18:2)

Section II – Temptation

Tests involve a choice to follow the righteous ways of God or to follow the influences of unclean spirits and/or those of the world. Tests assist us on our way towards perfection.

My brethren, count it for joy when you fall into various trials, knowing that the testing of your faith produces patience. But let patience have its perfect work, that you may be perfect and complete, lacking nothing. (James 1:2–4)

This perfect work is centered around our hearts, for our hearts reflect our faith.

You also be patient. Establish your hearts, for the coming of the Lord is at hand. (James 5:8)

The kingdom of heaven is a testing ground. It consists of many paths, each containing one or more obstacles. These obstacles are like rocks. Each rock represents one of the elements of the iniquitous nature that resides within every person. As the disciple encounters these rocks, that person is confronted with choices. A person may elect to walk around or step over the rock, yet the path is cleared if the disciple removes the rock. The condition of the mind and heart improves as these rocks are removed. If the disciple does not remove the rocks from the paths, the Lord may cause the disciple to return to the rocks until all the rocks that God wishes to be removed are cleared out. It is then that the believer has passed the test.

> ... But he who puts his trust in Me shall possess the land, and shall inherit My holy mountain. And one shall say, "Heap it up! Heap it up! Prepare the way, take the stumbling block out of the way of My people." (Isaiah 57:13, 14)

Life does not come to a halt if the disciple cannot remove the rock. Life continues, and the Lord is gracious to protect His own. The Lord will not force a disciple to remove a rock that is beyond his or her strength.

> No temptation has overtaken you except such as is common to man; but God is faithful, who will not allow you to be tempted beyond what you are able, but with the temptation will also make the way of escape, that you may be able to bear it. (1 Corinthians 10:13)

A disciple who continues in the Lord despite the obstacles will gain strength as he acquires the attributes of God. Faith increases as these attributes increase. This faith can build up enough so that the disciple not only removes a rock, but even a mountain.

> ... if you have faith as a mustard seed, you will say to this mountain, "Move from here to there," and it will move; and nothing will be impossible for you. (Matthew17:20)

People are given the freedom of choice; the Lord does not cause people to sin. It is by their own desire that they are drawn away to sin. When tempted by evil, God does not force us to fail or choose to sin.

> Let no one say when he is tempted, "I am tempted by God"; for God cannot be tempted by evil, nor does He Himself

tempt anyone. But each one is tempted when he is drawn away by his own desires and enticed. (James 1:13, 14)

Yet there is hope for those who remove the rocks that attempt to make them stumble. Those who endure temptation will be blessed by God.

Blessed is the man who endures temptation; for when he has been proved, he will receive the crown of life which the Lord has promised to those who love Him. (James 1:12)

If a disciple succumbs to temptation, that person gives birth to sin. Sin becomes fully grown when the disciple stumbles on many stones and no longer perseveres in spiritual growth. Full-grown sin eventually leads to death.

Then, when desire has conceived, it gives birth to sin; and sin, when it is full-grown, brings forth death. (James 1:15)

Section III – Perseverance

While wandering the paths of life in the kingdom of heaven, a disciple of Christ is confronted with attacks from the enemy from all directions. This enemy will consist of deception from evil spirits, lawlessness from the peoples of the earth, hate from friends and relatives, and persecution for his or her beliefs. Upon continuing in the faith and enduring to the end, the disciple will be saved and eternally rewarded.

Then they will deliver you up to tribulation and kill you, and you will be hated by all nations for My name's sake. And then many will be offended, will betray one another, and will hate one another. Then many false prophets will rise up and deceive many. And because lawlessness will abound, the love of many will grow cold. But he who endures to the end will be saved. (Matthew 24:9–13)

And you will be hated by all for My name's sake. But he who endures to the end will be saved. (Matthew 10:22)

While in the body of Christ, we must persevere to the end if we want to reach our goal.

> But Christ as a Son over His own house, whose house we are if we hold fast the confidence and the rejoicing of the hope firm to the end. (Hebrews 3:6)

> For we have become partakers of Christ if we hold the beginning of our confidence steadfast to the end. (Hebrews 3:14)

Some theologians will argue the point that John 3:16 ensures our salvation and that once saved, always saved. The wording in John 3:16 says that those who believe shall be saved. What exactly is "belief"? Believing in Jesus Christ is abiding in the vine, that is, dwelling in the kingdom of heaven. A person practicing lawlessness while in the body of Christ does not fully believe in the promise of God and will be cast into outer darkness, and those who remain will be presented to the Father. Salvation comes after enduring to the end. And yes, once in the Father's kingdom we are saved; and because it is eternal salvation, we are "always saved."

This means that the way to salvation is quite constrained and only a few have the strength to make it. Matthew 7 speaks of the narrow way to the kingdom of God.

> Enter by the narrow gate; for wide is the gate and broad is the way that leads to destruction, and there are many who go in by it. Because narrow is the gate and difficult is the way which leads to life, and there are few who find it. (Matthew 7:13, 14)

To be eternally separated from the presence of God is quite frightening. It's time for those who call themselves Christians to be concerned about their way of life!

Section IV – Spiritual Warfare

As many accounts in the gospels attest, evil spirits can dwell within the body. There are many examples found in Scripture in which evil spirits were cast out of people.

> When evening had come, they brought to Him many who were demon-possessed. And He cast out the spirits with a word, and healed all who were sick. (Matthew 8:16)

The power to cast out demons was not restricted to Jesus. His disciples were given the same power when they were sent out.

> Then the seventy returned with joy, saying, "Lord, even the demons are subject to us in Your name." (Luke 10:17)

The casting out of demons did not cease when Jesus departed from His disciples. Following His ascension, the apostles continued demonstrating this power to cast out demons.

> And the multitudes with one accord heeded the things spoken by Philip, hearing and seeing the miracles which he did. For unclean spirits, crying with a loud voice, came out of many who were possessed; and many who were paralyzed and lame were healed. (Acts 8:6, 7)

It is interesting to note that those who were sick, paralyzed, or lame were healed after demons were cast out. There is a direct association of various kinds of sicknesses with unclean spirits. Not all sicknesses or physical problems are caused or accompanied by unclean spirits. If someone falls out of a tree and breaks an arm, the broken arm is a result of the fall, not an unclean spirit. Many theologians will agree that spiritual conditions and sicknesses go hand in hand.

Accompanying Jesus' exorcisms, Jesus also makes a point that Christians are to deny the flesh. What is there about the flesh that draws this attention? Demons, being spirits, will influence the soul by various means of communication. In turn, demons will use the flesh to influence the soul. The existence of demons in the flesh cause sicknesses. In order to heal the sickness caused by demons, the demon associated with the sickness needs to be cast out first. If procedures such as the laying on of hands for healing are set in motion prior to the demon being cast out, there probably won't be a healing. The root of the problem—the demon—must first be dealt with before the symptom is remedied.

Demons are invited in by the sin that one commits. It is better to seek the spiritual cause of the sickness, cast it out, and then follow up with a physical healing by the laying on of hands. But a person is not free from the danger of the evil spirits coming back in. We must guard the gates of the city in order to prevent them from coming back in. Once driven away, one must not recommit the sin that has been forgiven. For if a person sins again, the latter state will be worse than the first.

> When an unclean spirit goes out of a man, he goes through dry places, seeking rest, and finds none. Then he says, "I will return to my house from which I came." And when he comes, he finds it empty, swept, and put in order. Then he goes and takes with him seven other spirits more wicked than himself, and they enter and dwell there; and the last state of that man is worse that the first... (Matthew 12:43–45)

When a person commits again the sin that was forgiven him, that person in a sense has prepared the way for the demon to return. The relationship of sinning and sickness is demonstrated in several New Testament verses.

> And behold, they brought to Him a paralytic lying on a bed. And Jesus, seeing their faith, said to the paralytic, "Son, be of good cheer; your sins are forgiven you."...For which is easier, to say, "Your sins are forgiven you," or to say, "Arise and walk"? (Matthew 9:2, 5)

This verse also demonstrates that it is better to deal with the root cause of the problem rather than the problem itself. The sequence of events to find true healing is to recognize the cause of the problem, seek the Lord's forgiveness, drive out the unclean spirit, and then lay hands on for healing.

Spirits that have a stronghold on a person are difficult to remove. Since they are of the flesh, fasting and praying for forgiveness of sins is one way to dislodge them. Fasting affects the flesh and in turn affects the grip that an unclean spirit has on a person.

> Then the disciples came to Jesus privately and said, "Why could we not cast him out?"... "However, this does not go out except by prayer and fasting." (Matthew 17:19, 21)

A believer freed from possession should always follow up with a prayer of thanksgiving upon being released from the grip of unclean spirits. This thanksgiving should not only be in mere words, but also in action with good intentions from the heart.

The promise offered us claims that the power of the Holy Spirit, when used in faith, will be enough to drive out the spirit. In the same breath, Jesus said:

> Because of your unbelief; for assuredly, I say to you, if you have faith as a mustard seed, you will say to this mountain, "Move from here to there," and it will move; and nothing will be impossible for you. (Matthew 17:20)

Notice the use of the mustard seed analogy. Faith does not come instantaneously. It grows like a mustard seed. We are to continue on our path to perfection. As we grow, our faith increases. In time, we will gather enough strength to drive out even the demons that require fasting and prayer as Jesus did.

The Lord Jesus Christ forgave and continues to forgive people of their sins. However, people still have iniquitous natures within themselves which need to be dealt with. This cleansing is performed daily.

> ... as Christ also loved the church and gave Himself for it, that He might sanctify and cleanse it with the washing of water by the word, that He might present it to Himself a glorious church... (Ephesians 5:25–27)

In the New Testament, casting out unclean spirits was as common as healing sicknesses. This same healing should be as common today. Churches need deliverance ministries, as the numbers of those seeking freedom from oppressive spirits is great.

The tendency of some Christians is to demand immediate correction of deformities or physical problems. While in some cases this takes place immediately and we call them miracles, other times it takes a long period of time. The Lord wants us to seek out our iniquities and deal with them. Once we have proven our sincerity by conquering the spiritual problem, then we are left with the physical evidence of the sin. The Lord may choose to remove the physical deformity or leave it as a reminder of what the results of turning from Him will be like if we choose to fall away. Whatever the reason, it is for our own good and should not be considered a form of punishment.

The soul needs to be strengthened. Spiritual warfare needs to be waged against such things as adultery, love of praise, fondness of contention, tiresome jealousy, wrath, and anger. We must arm ourselves with swords, which are the words of God. We must be properly trained in how to affectively use these swords to defeat the enemy. The robber needs to be cast out through the gates of the city, that is, our bodies.

> The thief does not come except to steal, and to kill, and to destroy... (John 10:10)

The soldier of Christ must put on the whole armor of God. Without proper training and weapons, the enemy will overcome you. Soldiers of Christ must protect against evil. They should let God dwell in their camps, and let His Spirit protect them. Let holy reason become a torch in your soul, burning the wood which is the entirety of sin.

If we're not careful, we become like the idols that we worship. When we come to Christ, these idols should be identified. As the idols are destroyed, our countenance begins to change. Our physical appearance begins to reflect the light of Christ.

But we all, with unveiled face, beholding as in a mirror the glory of the Lord, are being transformed into the same image from glory to glory, just as by the Spirit of the Lord. (2 Corinthians. 3:18)

If we follow a god that promotes such attributes as murder, torture, deception, lying, and thievery, then we worship Satan, for these are his characteristics. The God who created the heaven and the earth does not endorse these characteristics to draw mankind into the kingdom of heaven.

Section V – Fish

Having dealt with the spirit world, let's examine the fish of the sea and how it relates to our spiritual growth.

As mentioned earlier, fish move about with no direction. The sea consists of the nations of the world. Fish represent people in the sea of nations. Yet fish wander the waters, susceptible to being devoured. The disciples of Jesus, on the other hand, have direction, for they focus on the attributes of God and grow in Christ.

It is interesting to point out that when Jonah attempted to escape from God's will, he ended up in the belly of a great fish. Wherever the fish went, he went. He became subject to the ways of the world. Many people are trapped by the ways of the world.

There are an inordinate number of preachers who for some reason or another grow weary of serving the Lord. Many can be found resting in the world—or a large fish. The way of escape from the whale can be found in the book of Jonah.

When placed in a current, fish will foolishly tend to swim against the current, and hence the current influences their direction. Energy is spent trying to stay with the flow. If the water is like a sport, the fish will flow with baseball games, football games, tennis, swimming, or the Olympics. If the water is a video game, people can be found in video arcades or fixed in front of computers. If the flow is television, the fish becomes a couch potato. Excessive engagements in these waters become false ways of living—unfulfilling and pointless.

This is not to say that exercising is evil. Exercising is good for maintaining a healthy body. If the focus of exercise is to maintain a healthy body, then it is not an act of flowing with the world. It is an act of taking care of the temple—the body—that God grants us. But there is a limit as to what exercising can do for you, and an addiction to it can reap problems. Over-exercising may cause bodily harm and fatigue.

> But reject profane and old wives' fables, and exercise yourself rather to godliness. For bodily exercise profits little, but godliness is profitable for all things, having promise of the life that now is and of that which is to come. (1 Timothy 4:7, 8)

The Bible teaches that the true way of living is to acquire God's attributes and to exercise these attributes to improve self in order to set examples for others to follow. Disciples who are dedicated to God will face criticism because they do not flow with the fads and philosophies of the world.

> For to this end we both labor and suffer reproach, because we trust in the living God, who is the Savior of all men, especially of those who believe. (1 Timothy 4:10)

Section VI – Grumbling

As children of God, we are taught to obey, honor, and trust God without grumbling. God uses a grumble meter when He grades tests given to His disciples. When Moses led the children of Israel out of Egypt, the major cause for Israel's calamities was their grumbling.

In Exodus 17 the children of Israel murmured against Moses because of the lack of water.

> And the people thirsted there for water, and the people murmured against Moses, and said, "Why is it you have brought us up out of Egypt, to kill us and our children and our livestock with thirst?" (Exodus 17:3)

They didn't trust in the Lord to provide water for them. They preferred the bondage of Egypt—with the security of water. They failed in the area of trusting the Lord to provide for this basic need. However, in His mercy, the Lord provided water from the rock.

In Numbers 11:1, the Lord was once again displeased when the people complained about having to walk three days, and He sent fire to the outskirts of the camp. Later, in Numbers 11:4, 33, the Lord struck the people with a plague when they complained about not having meat. In 14:2, the children of Israel persisted to murmur against Moses and Aaron; they didn't want to enter Canaan for fear of the sword. The resultant punishment was forty years of wandering in the wilderness.

In 16:1–40 (rebellion of Korah), they rebelled against the authority of Moses and Aaron. The Lord struck the rebellious with death. Afterwards, in 16:41–50, some of those who remained alive murmured over the death of the people, and God struck them with a plague; 14,700 people died as a result.

Are the sons of God like the children of Israel? Will they resort to the ways of the world when they are separated from their parents? Will our children mow the lawn when told to do so—without grumbling? Will they do it on their own without being told?

God loves His children. In this love, He protects, provides, instructs, comforts, and restores us (Psalms 23). As children we need to accept this love and rely on it. We must actively thank the Lord and honor Him for His love as an act of worship. Psalms and Proverbs deal quite heavily in the area of love and worship.

Our children need to be taught to accept our love (protection, provision, instruction, comfort, and restoration) with pleasure. Grumbling while mowing the lawn is not actively thanking parents for their love. As children of God, we need to worship God. As children, we need to honor our parents. The Bible teaches us to honor our parents that things may go well with us.

Section VII – Worldly Festivities

Another way in which the world will infect the Christian Church is in the area of festivities, many of which have their roots in ancient

Babylon. One of the main downfalls of the early Christian Church was the introduction of pagan holidays. The reason given by the Church for this practice was to provide a compromise to the pagans in order to convert them to Christianity. However, once converted, the festivities continued within the Church with Christian names or events attached to them. These festivities are like a cancer to the Church. Some Christians will defend them as being a way to draw the world's attention to Christ. In reality, it is like fighting fire with fire—with no results. But a true Christian should not practice the evil ways of the world. Believers should not use evil to destroy evil.

If a Christian walks in the light of God's attributes, the ways of the world are not needed to bring the world to Christ. We must remember that the things of the world that influence us could become gods to us, and we become like the gods that we worship. Only God's attributes should be allowed to influence the true Christian.

> But then, indeed, when you did not know God, you served those which by nature are not gods. But now after you have known God, or rather are known by God, how is it that you turn again to the weak and beggarly elements, to which you desire again to be in bondage? You observe days and months and seasons and years. I am afraid for you, lest I have labored for you in vain. (Galatians 4:8–11)

The false ways of the world and the influence of unclean spirits create a dark atmosphere. The transition from the pressures of darkness to the freedom of light carries with it the pressure of change. To overcome this shift, the transition must be steady and at a pace adapted to the state a person is in at the time when the believer accepted Christ.

> I can do all things through Christ who strengthens me. (Philippians 4:13)

The closer one gets to the end of the transition period, the less pressure one will feel and the more sensitive a person becomes to experiencing the power of the Holy Spirit.

Section VIII – At Day's End

The battlefield consists of trials, tests, and tribulations.

... Knowing that tribulation produces perseverance; and perseverance, character; and character, hope. (Romans 5:3, 4)

One must remember that adversity is a great teacher and that people who travel on uneventful paths do not develop strength. We must fight the good fight and become humble people of excellent character.

And so ends the fifth day concerning that which is good and that which is evil.

So the evening and the morning were the fifth day. (Genesis 1:23)

Chapter 6

The Sixth Day

Section I – Made in the Image of God

The first five days of creation are the design and plan for the kingdom of heaven. The school has been completed—a school that gives everyone the opportunity to enter and become disciples of Jesus Christ our Lord and Savior. The students have access to knowledge and understanding of the ways of God, and they are encouraged to grow and bear fruit in an environment of testing and trials designed to build one's character.

The sixth day involves the implementation of the kingdom of heaven. This is where man is made into the image of God. This process is accomplished in two stages. One is the preparation of disciples to enter the kingdom. The other is the actual opening of the door to allow the disciples to enter. The door is open following the death and resurrection of our Lord Jesus Christ.

The sixth day reads as follows:

> Then God said, "Let the earth bring forth the living creature according to its kind: cattle and creeping thing and beast

of the earth, each according to its kind"; and it was so. And God made the beast of the earth according to its kind, cattle according to its kind, and everything that creeps on the earth according to its kind. And God saw that it was good. Then God said, "Let Us make man in Our image, according to Our likeness; let them have dominion over the fish of the sea, over the birds of the air, and over the cattle, over all the earth and over every creeping thing that creeps on the earth." So God created man in His own image; in the image of God He created him; male and female He created them. Then God blessed them, and God said to them, "Be fruitful and multiply; fill the earth and subdue it; have dominion over the fish of the sea, over the birds of the air, and over every living thing that moves on the earth." And God said, "See I have given you every herb that yields seed which is on the face of all the earth, and every tree whose fruit yields seed; to you it shall be for food. Also, to every beast of the earth, to every bird of the air, and to everything that creeps on the earth, in which there is life, I have given every green herb for food," and it was so. Then God saw everything that He had made, and indeed it was very good. So the evening and the morning were the sixth day. (Genesis 1:24–31)

The seven days of creation narrative concludes with Genesis 2:3. This narration is followed by the history of the creation of man, the Garden of Eden, beasts, and then a woman.

This is the history of the heavens and the earth when they were created, in the day that the Lord God made earth and the heavens, before any plant of the field was in the earth and before any herb of the field had grown. (Genesis 2:4, 5)

The sequence of events in the history of creation, Genesis 1, has plants and trees growing in Day 3, birds and fish arriving on the scene in Day 5, and living creatures being created prior to man in Day 6. The sequence of events in Genesis 2 has God creating man before any plant of the field was on the earth (verses 5–7), then planting a garden (verse 8), then creating living creatures (verse 19), and lastly creating Eve (verse 22). Why is the sequence of events different? The most likely explanation is that there are two timelines.

One timeline outlines the plan for the kingdom of heaven that is written in allegorical form. This timeline is the Alpha and the Omega—the design, plan, introduction, implementation, and end of the kingdom of heaven. The other timeline deals with the physical creation surrounding the introduction of Adam and Eve and the Garden of Eden.

Section II – Prosperity

As with the other five days, the passage addressing the sixth day ends with: "So the evening and the morning were the sixth day." This indicates that the sixth day continues to address "that which concerns good and evil."

Disobedience to God was the main reason that Adam and Eve were forced out of the Garden of Eden. As a result, God placed mankind in an environment in which they had to deal with this issue. If mankind obeyed God, they prospered. If they disobeyed God, this prosperity was removed.

> He turns rivers into a wilderness, and the watersprings into dry ground; a fruitful land into barrenness, for the wickedness of those who dwell in it. He turns a wilderness into pools of water, and the dry land into watersprings. There He makes the hungry dwell, that they may establish a city for habitation, and sow fields and plant vineyards, that they may yield a fruitful harvest. He also blesses them, and they multiply greatly; and He does not let their cattle decrease. (Psalm 107:33–38)

However, prosperity was not the answer to life. It was used to address the issue of disobedience. Solomon summed it up in Ecclesiastes as he acquired great wealth only to realize that all that he had was vanity. He concluded that the most valuable essence of life consisted of preaching and following the commandments of God.

"Vanity of vanities," says the preacher, "All is vanity." And moreover, because the Preacher was wise, he still taught the people knowledge; yes, he pondered and sought out and set in order many proverbs. The Preacher sought to find acceptable words; and what was written was upright...words of truth... Fear God and keep His commandments, for this is the whole duty of man. (Ecclesiastes 12:8–10, 13)

The sixth day opens up with God creating the beasts of the earth, which included cattle. Wealth was in the form of cattle, sheep, goats, and other livestock. Before He created man in His image, God set in place the ability for him to prosper.

Then God said, "Let the earth bring forth the living creature according to its kind: cattle and creeping thing and beast of the earth, each according to its kind"; and it was so. And God made the beast of the earth according to its kind, cattle according to its kind, and everything that creeps on the earth according to its kind. And God saw that it was good. (Genesis 1:24, 25)

Livestock has often been associated with wealth. God blessed Jacob with wealth, and when Jacob departed from Laban, he took his acquired wealth with him. This wealth consisted of livestock.

Thus the man (Jacob) became exceedingly prosperous, and had large flocks, female and male servants, and camels and donkeys. (Genesis 30:43)

In the book of Job, Job feared God and shunned evil. Because of his righteousness, God blessed him with ten children, seven thousand sheep, three thousand camels, five hundred yoke of oxen, five hundred donkeys, and a very large household.

As Christians, we must be careful how we handle prosperity. It is said that the love of money is the root of all evil.

For the love of money is a root of all kinds of evil, for which some have strayed from the faith in their greediness, and pierced themselves through with many sorrows. (1 Timothy 6:10)

Notice that it says, "The **love** of money is a root of all kinds of evil"; it does not say that money itself is evil.

But those who desire to be rich fall into temptation and a snare, and into many foolish and harmful lusts which drown men in destruction and perdition. (1 Timothy 6:9)

As Christians, we are allowed to have wealth. However, we must take dominion over the wealth and not let wealth rule over us. If wealth is misused, it will be taken away. When wealth becomes an idol, the idol will be destroyed. One of the curses bestowed upon ungodly men is poverty—the need to borrow money, and thus be indebted to others rather than free.

He shall lend to you, but you shall not lend to him; he shall be the head, you shall be the tail. (Deuteronomy 28:44)

Money should be man's servant, not his master. When one uses the aptly named MasterCard and pays interest, the card becomes the user's master. Members of the body of Christ must have dominion over their wealth and use it wisely.

Blessing through prosperity should not be a key factor in driving us to be Christians. We should not embark on a game of reward verses punishment, hoping to "earn" God's financial favor. Our obedience to God should be natural from the heart, not an attempt to reap wealth.

Section III – The Creation of Man

Following the creation of cattle, man is then created in the image of God.

"Then God said, "Let Us make man in Our image, according to Our likeness; let them have dominion over the fish of the sea, over the birds of the air, and over the cattle, over all the earth and over every creeping thing that creeps on the earth."

So God created man in His own image; in the image of God He created him; male and female He created them. Then God blessed them, and God said to them, "Be fruitful and multiply; fill the earth and subdue it; have dominion over the fish of the sea, over the birds of the air, and over every living thing that moves on the earth." (Genesis 1:26–28)

Given that Adam and Eve were the first people to be created, one might surmise that their creation took on the image of God, and that they walked in God's righteousness and joy in the Garden of Eden.

For the kingdom of God is… righteousness and peace and joy in the Holy Spirit. (Romans 14:17)

If God created man in His image, why did He begin with the plan of salvation and establish the kingdom of His Son? The answer lies in the depths of human nature. Although Adam and Eve walked in God's righteousness, they had the propensity to sin and the free will to choose between good and evil. In exercising this free will in dealing with the serpent who deceived them, Adam and Eve initiated the downfall of mankind. God knew that man's free will and the propensity to sin would lead to this downfall. Therefore, He prepared a plan of redemption beforehand. Mankind begins by walking in the joy and righteousness of God, but then he falls and has the opportunity to move back into this image by way of the kingdom of heaven.

This premise is supported by the reason that God made man in the first place.

… He gives to all life, breath, and all things. And He has made from one blood every nation of men to dwell on all the face of the earth, and has determined their preappointed times and the boundaries of their habitation, so that they should seek the Lord… (Acts 17:25–27)

Adam and Eve initially walked with God in the garden; they were not in a position where they had to seek Him. After the fall, mankind no longer walked with God in the garden. If they wanted to walk intimately with their Maker again, they had to seek Him. Seeking Him meant going through the process of redemption through repentance and entering the kingdom of heaven.

Knowing that mankind was going to fall, God created an environment to facilitate the process of redemption. This meant preparing mankind to enter the kingdom of heaven that was implemented after the death and resurrection of our Lord Jesus Christ.

Section IV – The Great Harvest

In the beginning there was one man. Was it God's intent to stop here? How about when there were two people on the earth? Should God have stopped there? Would all the energy put into creation be worthy of only two people?

Perhaps the twelve tribes of Israel were a more worthwhile goal. Now, that's a lot of people! However, the time for fulfilling God's will concerning mankind did not occur during Genesis or Exodus. The harvest will not occur until the end times, thousands of years later.

... the harvest is the end of the age... (Matthew 13:39)

So why is the Lord waiting so long to fulfill His purpose? It appears that the Lord is looking for a great harvest. The intent for the harvest to be great was established from the beginning.

... and in multiplying I will multiply your descendants as the stars of the heaven and as the sand which is on the seashore... (Genesis 22:17)

This concept of reaping a plentiful harvest was reiterated in the New Testament in Christ's own words.

Then He said to them, "The harvest truly is great, but the laborers are few; therefore pray the Lord of the harvest to send out laborers into His harvest." (Luke 10:2)

As mentioned in the parable of the wheat and the tares, the harvest consists of the sons of the kingdom. History was designed to support the reaping of a great harvest of souls at the time of the end.

Section V – Power and Authority

After creating man, God then stated the following:

> Let them have dominion over the fish of the sea, over the birds of the air, and over the cattle, over all the earth and every creeping thing that creeps on the earth... have dominion over the fish of the sea, over the birds of the air, and over every living thing that moves on the earth. (Genesis 1:26, 28)

As previously discussed, fish of the sea are the people, multitudes, and nations of the earth who move about with no direction. Christians are to have power and authority over the people of the world. They should not let the world dominate them.

Birds, as also mentioned, are symbolic of unclean spirits. Here again, Christians are to have dominion over unclean spirits. They are able to do so when they are filled with the Holy Spirit.

> Nevertheless do not rejoice in this, that the spirits are subject to you, but rather rejoice because your names are written in heaven. (Luke 10:20)

> But you shall receive power when the Holy Spirit has come upon you; and you shall be witnesses to Me in Jerusalem, and in all Judea and Samaria, and to the end of the earth. (Acts 1:8)

When nearly one hundred and twenty disciples assembled on the day of Pentecost, the Holy Spirit came upon them in an incredible display.

Now when the Day of Pentecost had fully come, they were all with one accord in one place. And suddenly there came a sound from heaven, as of a rushing mighty wind, and it filled the whole house where they were sitting. (Acts 2:1, 2)

When the Spirit fell upon them, they received power. With this power came authority. As they went out to minister, they used this God-given authority to cast out demons and used power to heal the sick.

And the multitudes with one accord heeded the things spoken by Philip, hearing and seeing the miracles which he did. For unclean spirits, crying with a loud voice, came out of many who were possessed; and many who were paralyzed and lame were healed. (Acts 8:6, 7)

This power and authority was not just over unclean spirits. It included "everything that moved on the earth." The authority of the saints was similar to that given to the "seventy" who were sent out by Christ with the intention of healing and preaching that the kingdom of God has come near them.

After these things the Lord appointed seventy others also, and sent them two by two before His face into every city and place where He Himself was about to go. Then He said to them… "and heal the sick who are there, and say to them, 'The kingdom of God has come near to you.'" (Luke 10:1, 2, 9)

When the seventy returned, they proclaimed news of their authority over demons.

Then the seventy returned with joy, saying, "Lord, even the demons are subject to us in Your name." (Luke 10:17)

Behold, I give you the authority to trample on serpents and scorpions, and over all the power of the enemy, and nothing shall by any means hurt you. (Luke 10:19)

When the twelve were sent out, they were also gifted with such authority, being told to cast out demons.

And as you go...cast out demons... (Matthew 9:36)

Today's Christians who receive the baptism of the Holy Spirit have access to this same power that the apostles were granted two millennia ago. However, the gifts associated with this power are meted out as determined by the Lord. There are diversities of gifts, ministries, and activities.

Now there are diversities of gifts, but the same Spirit. There are differences of ministries, but the same Lord. And there are diversities of activities, but it is the same God who works all in all. But the manifestation of the Spirit is given to each one for the profit of all: for to one is given a word of wisdom through the Spirit, to another a word of knowledge through the same Spirit, to another faith through by the same Spirit, to another the gift of healings by the same Spirit, to another the gifts of miracles, to another prophecy, to another discerning of spirits, to another different kinds of tongues, to another the interpretation of tongues. But one and the same Spirit works all these things, distributing to each one individually as He wills. (1 Corinthians 12:4–11)

The extent of this supernatural power is demonstrated by the last two witnesses mentioned in Revelation.

And I will give power to my two witnesses, and they will prophesy one thousand two hundred and sixty days, clothed in sackcloth. These are the two olive trees and the two lampstands standing before the God of the earth. And if anyone wants to harm them, fire proceeds from their mouth and devours their enemies. And if anyone wants to harm them, he must be killed in this manner. These have power to shut heaven, so that no rain falls in the days of their prophecy; and they have power over waters to turn them to blood, and to strike the earth with all plagues, as often as they desire. (Revelation 11:3–6)

The United States of America with its predominant Christian population has demonstrated its strength both in military power and economics. As Christianity fades in America, this strength will likewise fade. The power of entities such as the antichrists, elicit drugs, sexual immorality, atheists, and special interest groups not aligned with God's principles will strip Christian America's ability to dominate over the aimless fish of the sea.

Section VI – Antichrists

This power and dominion that God's people are granted extends over the beasts of the earth as well.

... Let the earth bring forth the living creature according to its kind... and beast of the earth... have dominion... over every living thing that moves on the earth. (Genesis 1:24, 28)

Living creatures and beasts include antichrists. Those who deny the Father and reject the Word of God are called antichrists. John warns us of the antichrists—those which are here and those that are to come.

Little children, it is the last hour; and as you have heard that the Antichrist is coming, even now many antichrists have come, by which we know that it is the last hour... Who is a liar but he who denies that Jesus is the Christ? He is antichrist who denies the Father and the Son. (1 John 2:18)

The antichrists are deceivers, for they oppose the true nature of Christ.

For many deceivers have gone out into the world who do not confess Jesus Christ as coming in the flesh. This is a deceiver and an antichrist. (2 John 7)

The deceiving antichrists are like devouring beasts. This great deception is pronounced in the prophecy concerning the beasts in Revelation 13 as it involves a counterfeit christ, hence the word *anti*christ. In order to deceive Christians who are well educated in Scripture and well established within the body of Christ, this deception has to be masterfully executed.

For false christs and false prophets will arise and show great signs and wonders, so as to deceive, if possible, even the elect. (Matthew 24:24)

The antichrist will come as a wolf in sheep's clothing. Hidden within the sea of nations, he will be working his great deception. Sethur, one of the twelve spies of Moses, means "the hidden one," and he was one of the ten who encouraged Moses not to enter Canaan—against God's will. The numeric value of his name is 666.

The following is a comparison of the Revelation 13 antichrist (the beast who rises from the sea) and our Lord Jesus Christ:

Christ... Antichrist

Christ	Antichrist
7-fold Spirit	7 heads (7 mountains or gov'ts)
10 commandments	10 horns with crowns
Father is God	Father is a god (Satan)
Came in the flesh	Comes from the sea (humanity)
Died on the cross	Suffered mortal head wound
Resurrected	Resurrected
Lion of Judah	Beast has a mouth of a lion
Authority from Father	Authority from dragon (Satan)
Shall judge the wicked	Kills the saints
Ministered 3 1/2 years	Will minister 3 1/2 years

Revelation 1:4 refers to Christ as He who is, was, and is to come. In Revelation 17:8, the beast is referred to as he who *was*, is *not*, and will come. It is interesting to note that in reference to the beast, the number 8 is associated with destruction, whereas with Christ, the number 8 is salvation. For both, the number 8 represents finality.

> And the beast that was, and is not, is himself also the **eighth** and is of the seven, and is going to perdition (*destruction*). (Revelation 17:11; bolded for emphasis; italics added)

> And it was granted to him to make war with the saints and to overcome them. And authority was given him over every tribe, tongue, and nation. And all who dwell on the earth will worship him, whose names have not been written in the Book of Life of the Lamb slain from the foundation of the world. (Revelation 13:7, 8)

The land from which the second beast rises up from consists of those who are under God's law—Israel. For it is Israel who will allow the antichrist to stand in the Holy Place. It was Israel who persecuted Christ and His followers, and Israel is still awaiting the arrival of the Messiah. In their failure to recognize Jesus as the Messiah, Israel will succumb to the deception of the false christ.

> Therefore when you see the abomination of desolation, spoken of by Daniel the prophet, standing in the holy place (whoever reads, let him understand), then let those who are in Judea flee to the mountains. (Matthew 24:15)

Section VII – Righteousness

Despite humanity's evil ways, God is gracious to provide an environment that provides for the needs of people and animals while man progresses in His plan of salvation.

> And God said, "See, I have given you every herb that yields seed which is on the face of all the earth, and every tree whose fruit yields seed; to you it shall be for food. Also,

to every beast of the earth, to every bird of the air, and to everything that creeps on the earth, in which there is life, I have given every green herb for food"; and it was so. (Genesis 1:29, 30)

Life on earth is dependent on the condition of God's people. If God's people obey Him and live in a righteousness manner, God is good to provide rain to allow the green herb to flourish. When God's people disobey Him, a drought sets in, the herb dies off, and life suffers. Disobedience is followed by God pulling back His hand of provision.

Section VIII – The Good Samaritan

The significant events that take place in biblical history include the introduction of Adam and Eve in a peaceful place, the fall of man and his struggle with good and evil, the institution of the law to lead man to Christ, the birth/death/resurrection of Christ, the fivefold ministry at work, and the final judgment.

One of the most influential stories that relates to this progression told by Jesus Christ is the parable of the good Samaritan. In contrast to traditional views, this parable can be viewed as an impressive allegory of the fall and redemption of mankind.

And behold, a certain lawyer stood up and tested Him, saying, "Teacher, what shall I do to inherit eternal life?" He said to him, "What is written in the law? What is your reading of it?" So he answered and said, "You shall love the Lord your God with all your heart, with all your soul, with all your strength, and with all your mind, and your neighbor as yourself." And He said to him, "You have answered rightly; do this and you will live." But he, wanting to justify himself, said to Jesus, "And who is my neighbor?" Then Jesus answered and said: "A certain man went down from Jerusalem to Jericho, and fell among thieves, who stripped him of his clothing, wounded him, and departed, leaving him half dead. Now by chance a certain priest came down that road. And when he saw him, he passed by on the other side. Likewise a Levite, when he arrived at the place, came and looked, and passed by on the other side. But a certain Samaritan, as he journeyed, came where he was. And when he saw him, he had compassion. So he went to him and bandaged his wounds, pouring on oil and wine; and he set him on his own animal, brought him to an inn, and took care of him. On the next day, when he departed, he took out two denarii, gave them to the innkeeper, and said to him, 'Take care of him; and whatever more you spend, when I come again, I will repay you.' So which of these three do you think was neighbor to him who fell among the thieves?" And he said, "He who showed mercy on him." Then Jesus said to him, "Go and do likewise." (Luke 10:25–37)

This parable provided a key answer to a question from the crowd. Jesus responded with the parable of the good Samaritan to a lawyer who had asked, "Teacher, what shall I do to inherit eternal life?" Jesus responded by asking him, "What is written in the law?" The lawyer responded with, "You shall love the Lord your God with all your heart, with all your soul, with all your strength, and with all your mind, and your neighbor as yourself."

This presents an interesting dichotomy of Scripture. On one hand, Jesus is the true way to eternal life. On the other hand, Jesus is saying that by following the above commandments, you may inherit eternal life. What gives here? How do we resolve this contradiction?

Let's see how Jesus resolves this apparent inconsistency with the parable of the good Samaritan. Jesus knew that the lawyer would be uneasy with His response. The lawyer, seeking assurance that he is justified by his reply to receive eternal life, asked the fateful question, "Who is my neighbor?" The lawyer, being a lawyer, is going to cross-examine himself and make sure that there is no loophole or escape clause that could deny him eternal life.

Jesus begins His parable: "A certain man went down from Jerusalem to Jericho." Jerusalem means "Possession of Peace" or is sometimes called the city of peace. Here Jerusalem represents the

Garden of Eden. The man represents Adam and Eve, or mankind, who left the Garden of Eden. This is fallen man.

Jericho is the lowest city on the earth (825 feet below sea level) and was a hedonistic resort area where Herod had built a vacation palace. The name Jericho means "fragrance," and it is the fragrant lure of sin that attracts mankind to the world. Jericho represents hell, or perhaps the world at its worse—chaos rather than peace.

On the way to Jericho, the man fell among thieves, who stripped him of his clothing, wounded him, and departed, leaving him near death. The thieves represent the influence of unclean spirits who rob the man of what dignity he has left, and the accuser, Satan, leaves him exposed for the sins that he committed. The pains of life are represented by the wounds. Being close to death, Satan is probably saying to God, "Is he not mine?"

As an example, you pick up the morning paper and on the front page the headlines read, "CEO of Dottcom Inc. arrested for embezzling $10 million." The next day you read that the CEO was addicted to cocaine and had an affair with his secretary. His wife is divorcing him. The CEO is now sitting at the side of the road stripped of his dignity and his sins are exposed to the world.

Switching back to the parable, just by chance a priest came walking down the road. When he saw the man, he passed by on the other side of the road. The priest symbolizes the law of Moses. It was not that the priest didn't want to help the man, but the law of Moses did not have the power to save him.

Likewise, a Levite, when he arrived at the place and saw the man, passed by on the other side of the road. Levites, from the tribe of Levi, were charged with the care of the sanctuary. They assisted priests and were judges, scribes, lawyers, gatekeepers, and musicians. Once again, the works of the Levite could not save the man. The law and its works offered no life-giving salvation.

> Where is boasting then? It is excluded. By what law? Of works? No, but by the law of faith. Therefore we conclude that a man is justified by faith apart from the deeds of the law. (Romans 3:27, 28)

Knowing that a man is not justified by the works of the law but by faith in Jesus Christ, even we have believed in Christ Jesus, that we might be justified by faith in Christ and not by the works of the law; for by the works of the law no flesh shall be justified. (Galatians 2:16)

Then a Samaritan—one rejected by the Jews—came along and helped the man on the side of the road. The Samaritan represents Christ.

Then the Jews answered and said to Him, "Do we not say rightly that You are a Samaritan and have a demon?" Jesus answered, "I do not have a demon; but I honor My Father, and you dishonor Me." (John 8:48, 49)

Jesus did not deny that he was a Samaritan, as he was from Nazareth, which is in Samaria. Because of the cultural and religious differences of the era, the Jews had no respect for Samaritans.

In the parable the Samaritan displayed the mind of Christ, showing mercy and compassion to the man on the side of the road. He begins his means of salvation by bandaging the man's wounds. Allowing Jesus to bandage him says that the man is accepting his help, repenting of his sins, and letting Jesus forgive him of his sins.

The Samaritan then anoints him with oil and wine. The wine cleanses the wound. Spiritually, the wine is the atoning blood or the knowledge of sin that stings at first but washes away the sin and purifies the soul, allowing God's Spirit to reside within us. The oil is soothing and brings comfort. The Holy Spirit is our comforter. Through his actions, the good Samaritan saves the man from death.

The Samaritan then set the man on his own animal and brought him to an inn. This reflects Jesus bearing the burden of our sins. The inn represents the Church. It is here that the man will grow in Christ and become like him. To facilitate this, the Samaritan handed two denarii to the innkeeper and said, "Take care of him." The innkeeper represents the pastor of the church, while the two denarii represent an equal amount knowledge and understanding of the ways of God. The pastor is to instruct his congregation with knowledge and understanding of God's ways.

The Lord spoke the following to Jeremiah about the importance of pastoral leadership:

> And I will give you shepherds according to My heart, who will feed you with knowledge and understanding. (Jeremiah 3:15)

After giving the two denarii to the innkeeper, the Samaritan said, "Whatever more you spend, when I come again, I will repay you." This speaks of the Lord's second coming.

Jesus finishes the narration by saying that the neighbor to him who fell among the thieves is the one who showed mercy, and He commands us to go and do likewise. Loving your neighbor as yourself cannot be fulfilled by addressing situations with the law and the works of the law. Therefore, the lawyer could not achieve eternal life without entering the kingdom of heaven. The spirits of compassion and mercy come from the heart, not from the law. This nature comes from salvation and obtaining the mind of Christ.

The way of peace is to walk back towards Jerusalem—the city of peace. The tree of life grows in Zion, the Garden of Eden. It is sad to see those who walk out of the inn and head back towards Jericho—towards destruction and certain death.

Christians who wish to love their neighbor as themselves should search for those on the side of the road, reach out, and invite them to receive Christ. For it is God's desire to show mercy on them, to bind their wounds, anoint them with oil, and to lead them back to Jerusalem.

The five central ingredients of the kingdom of heaven are shown in this parable: The two denarii represent knowledge and understanding, the inn represents a place where the man can learn the ways of God, the man is the disciple, the innkeeper represents the pastor of the church, and the road between Jerusalem and Jericho is the testing ground.

The lesson here is that what is written in Scripture is knowledge. Taking it to the level described above is an example of truly understanding what has been written and applying it.

Section IX – At Day's End

The first five days involved the design and plan for the kingdom of heaven. The sixth day involves the implementation of the kingdom of heaven and a day of gathering God's chosen people from Abraham's descendants and causing them to enter into the kingdom of heaven where they will be instructed in knowledge and understanding of God's ways. One must not construe Abraham's descendants as only being of the tribes of Israel. For Abraham's descendants are those in Christ from all creeds, nations, and races of the world.

> There is neither Jew nor Greek, there is neither slave nor free, there is neither male nor female; for you are all one in Christ Jesus. And if you are Christ's then you are Abraham's seed, and heirs according to the promise. (Galatians 3:28, 29)

On the sixth day, the disciple is fashioned into the image of God to become a humble servant and laborer for the eternal call through Jesus Christ, our Lord and Savior. This was the purpose of Christ coming in the flesh. He came to redeem Israel and change them into His image. However, He was not received by Israel as their Messiah.

> He came to His own, and His own did not receive Him. But as many received Him, to them He gave the right to become children of God, even to those who believe in His name: who were born, not of blood, nor of the will of the flesh, nor of the will of man, but of God. (John 1:11–13)

After his conversion, Paul felt uncomfortable over the fact that Israel rejected the opportunity to enter the kingdom of heaven. Paul wished he could spend more time with Israel on this matter. However, he was assigned as an apostle to the Gentiles.

For I could wish that I myself were accursed from Christ for my brethren, my kinsmen according to the flesh, who are Israelites, to whom pertain the adoption, the glory, the covenants, the giving of the law, the service of God, and the promises; of whom are the fathers and from whom, according to the flesh, Christ came, who is over all, the eternally blessed God. Amen. (Romans 9:3–5)

Each person must make a choice to enter the kingdom of heaven or to walk away. By dwelling in the kingdom of heaven, man can see how the first five days of creation are woven together to shape believers into the image of God. And so, this is the sixth event dealing with good and evil.

So the evening and the morning were the sixth day. (Genesis 1:31)

Chapter 7

The Seventh Day

Section I – The End of the Age

> Thus the heavens and the earth, and all the host of them, were finished. And on the seventh day God ended His work which He had done, and He rested on the seventh day from all His work which He had done. Then God blessed the seventh day and sanctified it, because in it He rested from all His work which God had created and made. (Genesis 2:1–3)

God has set things in order. The design of His Church, the kingdom of heaven, was completed in the first five days. On the sixth day, God implemented this plan for the kingdom of heaven. Here, the first five days are woven together to form man into the image of God. This action can be thought of as a fivefold ministry.

When Jesus appears, He generally speaks in a figurative sense. This is one way to identify His presence in Scripture. While in the flesh, He spoke many parables. When appearing in Revelation, we find Him speaking in symbols and types. When appearing in the beginning—all things being made through Him—we see the creation narration in symbols and types. The creation of the kingdom of heaven in the beginning was the *Alpha*.

> "I am the Alpha and Omega, the Beginning and the End," says the Lord. (Revelation 1:8)

> On the seventh day, Jesus hands His kingdom to the Father.

> The Son of Man will send out His angels, and they will gather out of His kingdom all things that offend, and those who practice lawlessness... then the righteous will shine forth as the sun in the kingdom of their Father. (Matthew 13:41, 43)

> Then comes the end, when He delivers the kingdom to God the Father, when He puts an end to all rule and all authority and power. For He must reign till He has put all enemies under His feet. (1 Corinthians 15:24, 25)

The handing of the kingdom to the Father at the end is the *Omega*. In reading the Genesis account, the documentation of this day does not end with the classic expression, "So the evening and the morning were the seventh day." It appears at this point that the Lord's work is complete in regards to dealing with good and evil.

Section II – Resurrection and Judgment

Prior to handing His kingdom to the Father, Jesus returns in what is commonly referred to as "The Second Coming." At this point in time, the first resurrection occurs, which is followed by the thousand year reign.

> Blessed and holy is he who has part in the first resurrection. Over such the second death has no power, but they shall be priests of God and of Christ, and shall reign with Him a thousand years. (Revelation 20:6)

However, God's rest is not complete until the last enemy is put under His feet.

For He must reign till He has put all enemies under His feet. (1 Corinthians 15:25)

The second resurrection takes place at the end of the thousand year reign at the time of the great white throne judgment.

Then I saw a great white throne and Him who sat on it... And I saw the dead... standing before God, and the books were opened... And the dead were judged according to their works... And anyone not found written in the Book of Life was cast into the lake of fire. (Revelation 20:11–15)

Those names found in the Book of Life are sons of God who will enter His kingdom for eternity.

Section III – The Saints

A particular group of people will reign with Christ during the thousand year period. This group consists of the saints who qualified to be in the kingdom of heaven.

And I saw thrones, and they sat on them, and judgment was committed to them. And I saw the souls of those who had been beheaded for their witness to Jesus and for the word of God, who had not worshiped the beast or his image, and had not received his mark on their foreheads or on their hands. And they lived and reigned with Christ for a thousand years. (Revelation 20:4)

Revelation 20:6 states that they shall rule as priests of God and of Christ, also pointing out that they were part of the first resurrection. This group includes such saints as the apostle John, for he included himself as one of the kings and priests in his opening statement in Revelation 1:

And He has made us kings and priests to His God and Father. (Revelation 1:6)

Among the saints are a group of people referred to as "the bride of Christ." The bride consists of wise virgins as portrayed in the parable of the ten virgins. The five wise virgins represented those who took the fivefold ministry seriously and kept their lamps full by continuing to grow and flourish in the Lord.

The marriage between Christ and the Church is alluded to in Paul's discussion on marriage in Ephesians:

> For we are members of His body, of His flesh and of His bones. "For this reason a man shall leave his father and mother and be joined to his wife, and the two shall become one flesh." This is a great mystery, but I speak concerning Christ and the church. (Ephesian 5:30-32)

The marriage appears to occur in Revelation 19, prior to the time when Satan is bound and the beginning of the thousand year reign, and could very well be part of the first resurrection mentioned at the end of Revelaton 20.

> Let us be glad and rejoice and give Him glory, for the marriage of the Lamb has come, and His wife has made herself ready. And to her it was granted to be arrayed in fine linen, clean and bright, for the fine linen is the righteous acts of the saints. (Revelation 19:7-8)

The bride appears as the Lamb's wife in Revelation 21:

> "Come, I will show you the bride, the lamb's wife." (Revelation 21:9)

Section IV – The One Hundred and Forty-Four Thousand

In examining prophecy, the only group referred to as virgins were the one hundred and forty-four thousand.

Then I looked, and behold, a Lamb standing on Mount Zion, and with Him one hundred and forty-four thousand, having His Father's name written on their foreheads... These are the ones who were not defiled with women, for they are virgins. These are the ones who follow the Lamb wherever He goes. They were redeemed from among men, being first fruits to God and to the Lamb. (Revelation 14:1, 4)

The word "virgins" and the fact that they follow the Lamb wherever He goes indicate a possible relationship to the bride of Christ.

Further into prophecy, we learn that the Groom—Christ—selects His bride. The selection of the bride took place sometime after the opening of the sixth seal in Revelation 6, during which the one hundred and forty-four thousand servants were sealed.

"Do not harm the earth, the sea, or the trees till we have sealed the servants of our God on their foreheads." And I heard the number of those who were sealed. One hundred and forty-four thousand of all the tribes of the children of Israel were sealed. (Revelation 7:3, 4)

At this point, we begin to see "A Tale of Two Women" --- a contrast between the Bride and the Harlot. The bride is sealed in chapter 7, displayed and redeemed in chapter 12, made ready in chapter 19, married in either chapter 19 or 20 and shown in chapter 21.

Now when the dragon saw that he had been cast to the earth, he persecuted the woman who gave birth to the male Child. But the woman was given two wings of a great eagle, that she might fly into the wilderness to her place, where she is nourished for a time and times and half a time, from the presence of the serpent. (Revelation 12:13, 14)

The harlot is described in chapter 17; her fall in chapter 18; and heaven exalts over her judgment in chapter 19.

"Come, I will show you the judgment of the great harlot who sits on many waters." (Revelation 17:1)

Again they said, "Alleluia! And her smoke rises up forever and ever!"'" (Revelation 19:3)

A description of the bride is found through the interpretation of the names of the twelve tribes mentioned in Revelation 7. The meaning of the tribes' names is as follows:

Judah –	praise
Reuben –	behold a son
Gad –	fortune
Asher –	happy
Naphtali –	wrestling
Manassis –	causing forgetfulness
Simeon –	hearing
Levi –	joined
Issacher –	reward
Zebulon –	dwelling
Joseph –	may God add children
Benjamin –	son of the right hand

Using the meanings of the names (in the order as listed in Revelation 7), the following interpretation reveals the nature of the bride:

The bride of Christ consists of those who praise God. They shall bear a son (behold, a son). Their fortune in life is happiness. They will wrestle with their old way of living and try to forget the past. They shall hear the word of God and be joined to the Bridegroom. Their reward is to dwell with Him. God will add children to the Son of the right hand (Bridegroom).

The following verse offers another description of the bride:

Now a great sign appeared in heaven: a woman clothed with the sun, with the moon under her feet, and on her head a garland of twelve stars. (Revelation 12:1)

"Clothed with the sun" means that she is clothed with the glory of the Father. The moon being a type of Christ means that she stands on the foundation of the Word of God. The twelve stars identify her with the apostolic ministry called out in Revelation 7. She had a son who is referred to as the male child:

And she bore a male Child who was to rule all nations with a rod of iron. And her Child was caught up to God and to His throne. (Revelation 12:5)

This is what the common biblical-era expression "behold, a son" refers to, for sons were highly valued. Other children were added as expressed by the meaning of the name Joseph—may God add children.

A description of the one hundred and forty-four thousand can be made by examining the meaning of the tribes' names. But why the number one hundred and forty-four thousand? What is significant about that number?

The answer seems to be centered around the numbers twelve and one thousand. One thousand could represent the one thousand year reign of Christ before He turns His kingdom over to the Father. The number one thousand could also mean a multitude of people. This would be consistent with the multitudes of four thousand and five thousand fed by Christ.

As for the value of twelve, the names of the twelve tribes identify the bride of Christ. In other cases twelve represents the twelve apostles or the apostolic ministry that the bride stands on. This would be in line with the description of the bride in Revelation 21.

Come, I will show you the bride, the Lamb's wife... and showed me the great city, the holy Jerusalem... she had a great and high wall with twelve gates... and names written on them, which are the names of the twelve tribes of the children of Israel... now the wall of the city had twelve foundations, and on them were the names of the twelve apostles of the Lamb. (Revelation 21:9, 10, 12, 14)

The temple was built on the foundation of the apostles.

Having been built on the foundation of the apostles and prophets, Jesus Christ Himself being the chief cornerstone, in whom the whole building being joined together, grows into a holy temple in the Lord, in whom you also are being built together for a habitation of God in the Spirit. (Ephesians 2:20–22)

Mathematically it adds up. A multitude of people (1000) identified as the bride of Christ (12) who abide in the apostolic ministry (12) make up the 144,000 (1000 x 12 x 12). Keep in mind, the 144,000 is symbolic of a multitude of believers, not necessarily a fixed number of believers. The bride consists of all those who qualify as wise virgins.

In Revelation 21, the bride is the city of Jerusalem, and the temple in the city of Jerusalem consists of the Father and the Son.

But I saw no temple in it, for the Lord God Almighty and the Lamb are its temple. (Revelation 21:22)

Each of these prophecies offers believers deeper insight into what to expect. It is crucial that we embrace spiritual understanding so that we might be prepared for what is to come.

Section V – At Day's End

On the seventh day, Jesus hands His kingdom to the Father.

For He must reign till He has put all enemies under His feet. Then comes the end, when He delivers the kingdom to God the Father, when He puts an end to all rule and all authority and power. (1 Corinthians 15:24, 25)

Leading up to this event is the harvest and the thousand year reign. The one signpost that points to the time of the great harvest is the return of the Jews to Israel. Anti-Semitism, among other reasons, is driving hundreds of thousands of Jews out of Russia and other countries. This event was foretold by the prophet Jeremiah.

> "Therefore, behold, the days are coming," says the Lord, "that they shall no longer say, 'As the Lord lives who brought up the children of Israel from the land of Egypt,' but, 'As the Lord lives who brought up and led the descendants of the house of Israel from the north country and from all the countries where I had driven them.' And they shall dwell in their own land." (Jeremiah 23:7, 8)

As there are physical Jews ready to be harvested and returned to physical Israel, there are spiritual Jews ready to be harvested and brought into the body of Christ. It won't be long before the latter rain shall fall, and the harvest will be ready.

Prior to the birth of Christ, God's chosen people lived under the law, as represented by the tabernacle of Moses. Following Christ's ascension, God's chosen people were allowed to live under the law of liberty, as represented by the tabernacle of David.

A great restoration movement will soon come upon the earth. The one hundred and forty-four thousand will be sealed. There will be great tribulation as foretold in the book of the Revelation of Jesus Christ. Following the first resurrection, those who qualify will reign with Christ as kings and priests during the thousand year reign. After this comes the opportunity to drink of the river of eternal life.

> Blessed are those who do His commandments, that they may have the right to the tree of life. (Revelation 22:14)

Chapter 8

Conclusion

The previous chapters have opened up a different perspective on the seven days of creation. The seven days are summarized as follows:

First Day	The introduction of knowledge and understanding of the ways of God
Second Day	The creation of a school where disciples can acquire that which was provided on the first day
Third Day	The creation of a plan to give disciples an opportunity to enter the school
Fourth Day	The creation of authority and school administration
Fifth Day	The creation of a background to test disciples of Christ
Sixth Day	The weaving together of the first five days to change a person into the image of God
Seventh Day	The day when the Lord Jesus Christ hands His kingdom to the Father

In summary, the first five days of creation are the design and plan of the kingdom of heaven. The sixth day is the introduction and implementation of the kingdom of heaven. The seventh day is when the kingdom is handed to the Father. This aspect of the seven days is charted below:

First Five Days	Design & Plan for the Kingdom of Heaven
Sixth Day	Introduction & Implementation of the Kingdom of Heaven
Seventh Day	Handing of the Kingdom of Heaven to the Father

You have been presented with a purpose for living and made aware of an opportunity to receive an eternal life of peace and contentment. For those who choose to exercise this opportunity, the first five days of creation provide a pattern that allows one to acquire and implement God's character in his or her life.

Given that the Lord designed, planned, introduced, and implemented the kingdom of heaven, one cannot ignore its importance. The Lord does not want us continually standing around socializing in the outer court of the tabernacle. He wants us to go all the way to the Holy of Holies where we can worship the Lord in spirit and truth, hearing the word, and growing in Christ. Remember, faith without works is dead.

I encourage you to seek after the attributes of God, apply them, and in turn, offer the opportunity to receive eternal life to others. Remember that knowledge of these attributes is found in Jesus Christ; it is through our Lord Jesus Christ that we are able to know God the Father.

To truly grow in righteousness requires wisdom. Wisdom will come when the Holy Spirit of truth is allowed to enter and add understanding concerning God's ways. A proper balance of knowledge and understanding will create the wisdom that is needed in order to become a powerful member and servant within the body of Christ.

> Wisdom has built her house, she has hewn out her seven pillars; she has slaughtered her meat, she has mixed her wine, she has also furnished her table. She has sent out her maidens, she cries out from the highest places of the city, "Whoever is simple, let him turn in here!" As for him who lacks understanding, she says to him, "Come, eat of my bread and drink of the wine which I have mixed. Forsake foolishness and live, and go in the way of understanding." (Proverbs 9:1–6)

To the unbeliever whose heart and mind is clouded by the surrounding darkness, I beg that you repent of your sins and accept Jesus Christ as your Savior. In Him is life. Let His light shine brightly in your heart and mind. You have nothing to lose and everything to gain. Don't reject it until you have at least tasted of its pleasures.

To the young in Christ, I caution you to walk carefully. For deception is reaching out from every dark place, trying to grab hold of what little you have. Do not forsake gathering together in a local church. The church is like a ship riding on the sea of nations. The logos will serve as your guide and rudder. Rhema will provide the wind for your sails. Search for the ship that sails the seven seas of creation. It is this ship that will find the fountain of youth.

To those who have attained enough knowledge to make themselves dangerous, not only to themselves but to others as well, I implore that you give careful consideration to what has been written. Study the Scriptures. Weigh all matters fairly. Let the Holy Spirit lead you in the way of righteousness.

To the old men in Christ, I respectfully submit to you in all humbleness. However, I urge you to keep an eye on the cloud, for when the cloud moves, one should be prepared to weigh anchor and follow it.

Now may the God of peace who brought up our Lord Jesus from the dead, that great Shepherd of the sheep, through the blood of the everlasting covenant, make you complete in every good work to do His will, working in you what is well pleasing in His sight, through Jesus Christ, to whom be glory forever and ever. Amen. (Hebrews 13:20, 21)

About the Author

Dana George Cottrell was born in St. Stephen, New Brunswick, Canada and was raised in northern Maine. He graduated from the University of Maine with a bachelor of science degree in electrical engineering, and he holds a master of arts degree in biblical studies from the Mission Bay Christian Fellowship School of Ministries in San Diego, California.

This book, with its unique interpretation of the seven days of creation, was formulated from a compilation of divine revelation, his own insights, individual research, sermons, and classroom instruction.